Gunfighters of the American West

Other Books in the History Makers Series:

Gunfighters of the American West

By Thomas Thrasher

Lucent Books
P.O. Box 289011, San Diego, CA 92198-9011

978
THR

Library of Congress Cataloging-in-Publication Data

Thrasher, Thomas, 1968–
    Gunfighters of the American West / by Thomas Thrasher.
        p.   cm. — (History makers series)
    Includes bibliographical references and index.
    Summary: Discusses six famous and influential American gunfighters,
including "Wild Bill" Hickok, Wyatt Earp, and William H. "Billy The Kid"
Bonney
        ISBN 1-56006-570-2 (lib : alk. paper)
        1. Outlaws—West (U.S.) Biography—Juvenile literature.   2. Peace
Officers—West
(U.S.) Biography—Juvenile literature.   3. Frontier and pioneer life—West
(U.S.)—Juvenile literature.   4. West (U.S.) Biography—Juvenile literature.
[1. Peace officers. 2. Robbers and outlaws. 3. West (U.S.) Biography.]
I. Title.   II. Series: History makers.
    F594.T52   2000
    978'.02'0922—dc21   99-27132
[B]
CIP

Cover: Center: Billy the Kid; Clockwise from top right: James B. Hickok;
Wyatt Earp; John Wesley Hardin; Tom Horn

Printed in the U.S.A.

CONTENTS

FOREWORD

The literary form most often referred to as "multiple biography" was perfected in the first century A.D. by Plutarch, a perceptive and talented moralist and historian who hailed from the small town of Chaeronea in central Greece. His most famous work, *Parallel Lives*, consists of a long series of biographies of noteworthy ancient Greek and Roman statesmen and military leaders. Frequently, Plutarch compares a famous Greek to a famous Roman, pointing out similarities in personality and achievements. These expertly constructed and very readable tracts provided later historians and others, including playwrights like Shakespeare, with priceless information about prominent ancient personages and also inspired new generations of writers to tackle the multiple biography genre.

The Lucent History Makers series proudly carries on the venerable tradition handed down from Plutarch. Each volume in the series consists of a set of five to eight biographies of important and influential historical figures who were linked together by a common factor. In *Rulers of Ancient Rome*, for example, all the figures were generals, consuls, or emperors of either the Roman Republic or Empire; while the subjects of *Fighters Against American Slavery*, though they lived in different places and times, all shared the same goal, namely the eradication of human servitude. Mindful that politicians and military leaders are not (and never have been) the only people who shape the course of history, the editors of the series have also included representatives from a wide range of endeavors, including scientists, artists, writers, philosophers, religious leaders, and sports figures.

Each book is intended to give a range of figures—some well known, others less known; some who made a great impact on history, others who made only a small impact. For instance, by making Columbus's initial voyage possible, Spain's Queen Isabella I, featured in *Women Leaders of Nations*, helped to open up the New World to exploration and exploitation by the European powers. Unarguably, therefore, she made a major contribution to a series of events that had momentous consequences for the entire world. By contrast, Catherine II, the eighteenth-century Russian queen, and Golda Meir, the modern Israeli prime minister, did not play roles of global impact; however, their policies and actions significantly influenced the historical development of both their own countries and their regional neighbors. Regardless of their relative importance in the greater historical scheme, all of the figures chronicled in the History Makers series made contributions to posterity; and their public achievements, as well as what is known about their private lives, are presented and evaluated in light of the most recent scholarship.

In addition, each volume in the series is documented and substantiated by a wide array of primary and secondary source quotations. The primary source quotes enliven the text by presenting eyewitness views of the times and culture in which each history maker lived; while the secondary source quotes, taken from the works of respected modern scholars, offer expert elaboration and/or critical commentary. Each quote is footnoted, demonstrating to the reader exactly where biographers find their information. The footnotes also provide the reader with the means of conducting additional research. Finally, to further guide and illuminate readers, each volume in the series features photographs, two bibliographies, and a comprehensive index.

The History Makers series provides both students engaged in research and more casual readers with informative, enlightening, and entertaining overviews of individuals from a variety of circumstances, professions, and backgrounds. No doubt all of them, whether loved or hated, benevolent or cruel, constructive or destructive, will remain endlessly fascinating to each new generation seeking to identify the forces that shaped their world.

Gunfighters of the American West

Thanks to Hollywood and cheap novels, the image that many people have of gunfights is a duel between a "good guy" and a "bad guy" on a dusty frontier street at high noon. However, the stand-up gunfight in the American West was more the exception than the rule. The majority of gunfights were drunken affairs in saloons fought over women, gambling, or insults. Combatants rarely dueled but, instead, tried to get the "drop" on their opponents and catch them at a disadvantage.

A gunfighter is defined in this book as someone who killed an equally armed opponent but not during the commission of a crime. There is a huge difference, for example, between killing an unarmed bank clerk during a bank robbery and shooting an armed gambler during a quarrel over a card game. For this reason, outlaws such as Jesse James and Kid Curry have been omitted while figures such as Wild Bill Hickok and Billy the Kid have been included.

James Butler Hickok, otherwise known as "Wild Bill," was a legend in his own time, and since then the legend has grown. He has come to be regarded as the yardstick against which other gunslingers are measured. People who know nothing else about the history of the American West are often familiar with the name of Wild Bill Hickok.

"Billy the Kid," whose real name was William Bonney, is another gunfighter whose name is instantly recognizable. Dead by the age of twenty-one, Bonney killed seven people during the course of a conflict known as the Lincoln County War. Like Hickok, Billy the Kid has become a part of the gunfighter legend.

Ben Thompson, although not as famous as Billy the Kid or Wild Bill Hickok, was no less competent with firearms. Considered by some to be a "gunfighter's gunfighter," Thompson's life in many ways embodies the western experience. He saw combat in the Civil War, worked as a mercenary in Mexico, served time for mur-

Wyatt Earp's participation in the gunfight at the O.K. Corral in Tombstone, Arizona, is only one of his claims to fame as pictured here in a scene from a movie.

der in Texas, ran a saloon in Kansas, and became the marshal of Austin, Texas.

Wyatt Earp is another legendary gunslinger, although he rarely used his gun. Earp was the marshal of Dodge City, Kansas, but is better known for his participation in the shootout at the O.K. Corral in Tombstone, Arizona. Earp eventually became a Los Angeles police officer and married a wealthy widow. He died in his sleep in 1929.

The most prolific gunfighter of the American West in terms of victims was John Wesley Hardin. This son of a Methodist preacher is reputed to have slain a man just for snoring. By the time he had turned twenty, Hardin was documented as having killed twenty-one men. He was eventually captured and spent seventeen years in prison, where he earned a degree in law. Upon his release from prison, Hardin opened a law office.

Tom Horn is considered to be the last of the gunfighters. A former army scout and Pinkerton detective, Horn was executed in

1903 for the murder of a fourteen-year-old boy. Horn's death signaled a change in the public's attitude about "frontier justice" and marked the end of the gunfighter's era.

The image of the gunfighter in movies, on television, and in cheap novels is not accurate. These fictionalized portrayals ignore the gunfighters' alcoholism, sensationalize the violence, simplify the conflicts into battles between good and evil, and trivialize death. The gunfighter was neither hero nor villain. He was, however, a part of the history of the American West.

CHAPTER 1

America's Westward Expansion

The settlement of the American West is one of the key elements in the history of the United States. The idea of a "frontiersman," an individual willing to face unknown odds alone, has always appealed to the American imagination and the belief in individual initiative. With the westward expansion of the United States almost from the time of the first settlement in Jamestown, Virginia, the West became a mythic realm in which anything was possible if one tried hard enough.

The single most important event in the expansion of the United States came in April 1803 when President Thomas Jefferson paid France $15 million for the area west of the Mississippi River then known as Louisiana. This one purchase doubled the size of the young nation. In the summer of 1803, Jefferson dispatched an expedition led by Meriwether Lewis and William Clark to explore the newly purchased region. The journey of Lewis and Clark took three years, but their report fanned public interest in the West and demonstrated the feasibility of an overland route to the Pacific Ocean.

America continued to expand and added the Florida Territory in 1819. Texas, formerly part of Mexico, was annexed in 1845, leading to war with Mexico from 1846 to 1848. As a result of losing that war, Mexico was forced to cede California and the New Mexico Territory to the United States in 1848. Meanwhile, the Oregon Territory in the Northwest was added to the Union after negotiations with Great Britain in 1846. This last acquisition perfected the American dream of "Manifest Destiny."

"Manifest Destiny" was a term coined by the editor of the *Democratic Review* in 1845. It refers to the belief that, because American institutions and cultures were thought to be superior to those of its Native American and Hispanic neighbors, the United States was destined to control the entire North American continent, from the Atlantic to the Pacific.

A group of settlers moves west to begin a new life, greatly shaping the country's history.

Once war and diplomacy had finalized the status of the western territories, Americans lost little time in moving there. The westward migration began as a trickle in the 1840s and grew into a flood by the 1870s. Americans, as well as immigrants from Europe, made the trek west in search of opportunities that could not be found in the crowded urban centers of the East. Some came in search of land or gold; others were hoping the West would restore their physical health; still others were pursuing freedom to practice their religious beliefs. There were also those who came in search of adventure.

Although many moved west in search of a better life, there were those who were drawn to the West by the promise of quick riches at the expense of others and by opportunities afforded by lax law enforcement. This criminal element was not just restricted to robbers and livestock rustlers but included forgers, land speculators, gamblers, gunrunners, and swindlers of every stripe.

A Violent Society

This lack of law enforcement allowed a violent society to flourish. A man had to be prepared to defend his family and home on his own since help was often miles away, if it existed at all. Richard Maxwell Brown, a noted historian of the American West, attributes the prevalence of violence in the West in part to the doctrine of "no duty to retreat." English common law (from which American law is descended) held that a person threatened with violence had to retreat as far as possible, "to the wall" at one's back, before violently resisting an antagonist. As Americans moved west, however, courts in state after state turned the English "duty to retreat" on its head and replaced it with the principle of "no duty to retreat." An Ohio court, for example, ruled that a "true man . . . [was] not obligated to fly" from an assailant. In another case, the Indiana Supreme Court ruled that "the tendency of the American mind seems to be very strongly against the enforcement of any rule which requires a person to flee when assailed."[1]

Going hand in hand with the idea of no duty to retreat was the notion of self-redress for grievances and an ideology of vigilantism. The idea of personally seeking revenge for wrongs was deeply ingrained in the American mind, especially in the South. Likewise, the ideology of vigilantism, taking the law into one's own hands for the purpose of enforcing the law, was well entrenched in American values.

The homestead ethic and the ethic of individual enterprise were two competing ideas that also caused bloodshed. The homestead ethic dated back to colonial America and can be boiled down to a belief in three rights: the right to own a family-sized farm, the homestead; the right to a homestead unencumbered by oppressive taxes; and the right to occupy the homestead without the threat of violence. The ethic of individual enterprise, on the other hand, maintained that a company or an individual needed to be aggressive in order to carve out, maintain, and expand a place in the economy. According to this ethic, it was acceptable to use violence to defend, and in some cases to expand, one's commercial interests. In the American West, these two competing ethics led to range wars, blood feuds, and gun battles.

Many of these ideas found their best expression in the "Code of the West." Nineteenth-century America was obsessed with the idea of masculine honor, and the Code of the West was a variant of this idea. Central to the Code of the West were the ideas of no duty to retreat, self-redress for wrongs, and personal courage. In a variation of this code, an Englishman who traveled across the American West between 1870 and 1880 described the "cowboy code of honor" as "honesty, courage, sensitive pride, stoic indifference to pain, and, above all, a violent vengefulness against insult."[2]

How the West Was Settled

Setting out from Independence, Missouri, a stream of settlers flowed west, bringing with them their systems of beliefs. As the number of settlers grew, small towns, forts, and outposts were established along the major overland routes to serve, protect, and occasionally swindle the pioneers. During the California gold rush of 1849, these towns provided services to would-be miners rushing to what they believed were future fortunes; they also traded supplies for pelts with trappers and buffalo hunters. As cities in the East grew, they began to demand more beef than could be raised on small eastern farms, and cattle therefore became a valuable commodity. In the open spaces of the West, the cattle industry was born.

The flow of settlers to the West contributed to, and was temporarily slowed by, one of the most momentous events in American history: the Civil War. In the West, the Civil War took the form of guerrilla warfare. In fact, more than one gunfighter learned, or perfected, his skills during the Civil War. Wild Bill Hickok served as a scout in the Union army, and Ben Thompson

Frontier life was harsh and full of violence, mostly due to a lack of law enforcement.

Cattle are rounded up for shipment to Kansas. These men led the way into the cowboy era.

served in the Confederate cavalry. John Wesley Hardin, although too young to have taken part in the war, recalled that he saw Lincoln "burned and shot to pieces in effigy so many times. I looked upon him as a demon incarnate."[3] With the Civil War, a generation of men became inured to the idea of casual violence.

During the Civil War, the Union army cut off Texas from its beef markets in the Confederacy. As a result, the herds were abandoned and some of the longhorn cattle became wild. By the end of the Civil War, an estimated 5 million longhorns roamed the Texas grasslands and were free to the man who dared to rope and brand them. The cattle were rounded up by groups of men and driven north from Texas to the stockyards and rail depots in Kansas. The era of the cowboy had begun.

Following the war, many men without homes or families drifted west in search of new lives. Although a man might easily find work as a cowboy, it was a hard life. Months might pass in which he would not see a town or associate with anyone but his fellow cowboys. After months on the trail, the Texas cowboys would finally arrive in a Kansas town, sell the cattle, and then "hurrah" the town by racing down the main street firing their Colt revolvers into the air.

The Weapons That Won the West

The weapons a cowboy carried were as important to him as his horse. It was said in the American West that "God made man, but Sam Colt made all men equal."[4] Samuel Colt was a sailor who got the idea for the "revolver" after watching the steering wheel on a ship at sea and noticing how it "clicked" into position. He first patented his idea in Britain and then in the United States in 1835. Colt's "revolving" pistol allowed a person to shoot multiple times without reloading, a feature that provided a distinct advantage in combat. Colt's .44 caliber single-action revolver became the favorite weapon of gunfighters throughout the American West ("single-action" means that the hammer of the gun needed to be pulled back with the thumb before the gun could be fired). Some people referred to the gun as "Judge Colt and his jury of six."[5]

Colt applied his revolver idea to rifles and shotguns as well, and he had a fair amount of success until Christopher Spenser came along. A lifelong inventor, Spenser designed a seven-shot lever-action repeating rifle that saw service in the Civil War and later in the wars between whites and Native Americans. The company that Spenser sold his design to was taken over by New Haven

The invention of the Colt revolver allowed gunfighters to shoot multiple times without reloading.

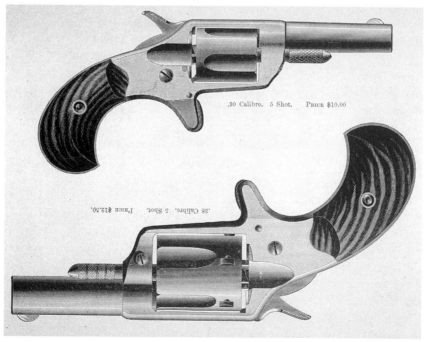

Arms Company in 1857. A man there named B. Tyler Henry was chosen by his superior, Oliver F. Winchester, to manage the repeating rifle operation. Henry redesigned the ammunition and the rifle so that its magazine capacity was increased to sixteen rounds. Oliver Winchester, in turn, refined Henry's design to make the lever and firing action smoother and placed a "receiver" slot on the side of the rifle for easier loading. The Winchester model of 1866, and the slightly modified model of 1873, became the favorite rifle among settlers in the West. Because of its popularity, some people even claim that it is the "gun that Won the West."[6]

The improved accuracy and magazine capacity of the firearms contributed to the culture of violence in the West. The accuracy of the new weapons made it possible to hit a target at unheard-of distances. Furthermore, the increased magazine capacity made it possible to fire a weapon repeatedly without reloading. These two advances had the effect of giving each man the firepower of a miniature army.

Although advances in firearms were among the chief elements of the violence of the times, alcohol abuse also played a role. In many frontier towns, alcohol laws were either nonexistent or unenforced. Beer and hard liquor were available twenty-four hours a day, seven days a week. Many of the men who frequented the saloons in the West were fresh from the trail, down from the mountains, or on leave from the army, and they would indulge in binge drinking. Under the influence of alcohol, these proud, independent men would fight at the slightest provocation.

Like laws governing alcohol, firearm laws were either nonexistent or unenforced in many western towns. For example, there were no restrictions placed on the purchase of firearms. Anyone, of any age, could purchase a gun with no questions asked. Not only were firearms easy to buy, but they could also be carried openly, and many men chose to exercise this privilege.

As might be expected, freely available alcohol and firearms often proved to be a lethal combination. John B. Edwards, an early resident of Abilene, Kansas, noted that cowboys were likely to get "too much tanglefoot aboard [get drunk]" and were "liable under the least provocation to use [their] navies [six-shooters], of which not less than one or two were always hanging from their belts. In fact, if their fancy told them to shoot, they did so, in the air, at anything they saw and a plug hat would bring a volley at any time from them, drunk or sober."[7] Many gunfighters, on both sides of the law, earned their reputations in drunken, often deadly, brawls.

The era of the gunfighter in American history began with Wild Bill Hickok in 1861, the year the Civil War began, but it did not reach its zenith until after the end of the Civil War. The period 1870–1880 accounts for most of the violence associated with professional gunmen. In 1890, the federal government declared the frontier "closed," but by then gunfights were quickly becoming a thing of the past and were restricted to isolated areas of the American West. Tom Horn's execution in 1903 marks the end of the age of the gunfighter and the beginning of the public's intolerance for wanton violence and professional killers.

CHAPTER 2

The Prince of the Pistoleers: James Butler "Wild Bill" Hickok

"The Prince of the Pistoleers," James Butler Hickok, the fourth of six children, was born on May 27, 1837, on a farm in La Salle County, Illinois. His father, William Alonzo Hickok, was a farmer who also operated a general store that was used as a hideout to house escaped slaves until they could be smuggled to safety farther north. James's mother, Polly Butler Hickok, came from a well-to-do New England family and raised the Hickok children to believe in God and in themselves. She made sure that her children received the best education possible.

Hickok family tradition asserts that James displayed a liking for the outdoors at an early age and that he preferred hunting game for the family's dinner to pushing a plow, chopping wood, or other chores. James participated in his father's antislavery activities as well by helping guide escaping slaves north. The Hickok family claims that James heard his first shot fired in anger when he and his father were chased and fired upon by bounty hunters while helping guide a group of escaped slaves north.

Although he was willing to help his father, James had no interest in being a farmer. After William Hickok died in March 1852, James Hickok let it be known that he intended to leave the family farm and head west. At fifteen years of age, James was man-size and was already expressing his independence. Three years later, James and his brother Lorenzo left La Salle County bound for Kansas.

The circumstances of their departure are uncertain. According to one story, following a brawl with a teamster named Charlie Hudson, whom he beat into unconsciousness, James fled with his brother Lorenzo, fearing that he had killed Hudson. However, it is just as likely that the brothers were escaping the boredom of the family farm and their overbearing mother for the excitement of the West. Whatever the reason, James returned home only once, for a brief visit in 1869.

Hickok in the West

What is known is that in 1858, James Hickok, although only twenty-one years old, was deemed tough enough to be made one of the four

constables protecting the citizens of Monticello township in the Kansas Territory. The job, however, was less exciting than James had hoped, and he left Monticello in 1859 with a freighting outfit bound for Colorado. By his own account it was during this expedition that Hickok was mauled by a black bear, which he killed after emptying two six-shooters into it and stabbing it repeatedly. Like other stories that Hickok told about himself, this one should be viewed suspiciously because there is no one to confirm the tale and Hickok was known to embellish the truth when it suited him.

James Hickok was one of the first to make a name for himself as a gunfighter.

Hickok's next two years are a mystery, but by 1861 he was employed with the Overland Stage Company as a stock tender (the person who would feed and water the company's livestock). It was while working in this capacity at the East Rock Creek Station in the Nebraska Territory that James Hickok experienced a defining event in his life. On July 12, 1861, Hickok killed his first man, David McCanles, under suspicious circumstances.

Hickok's version of events differed substantially from the official story. Court records from the time indicate that David McCanles, a brawny, fiery Southerner, had sold the East Rock Creek Station to the company of Wolfe and Hagenstien with the agreement that the purchase price of $1,200 would be paid in full a year later. When the date for the payment fell due, McCanles went to the station to collect the money but was told by the station-master, Horace Wellman, that the money had not yet arrived and that Wellman would need to travel to the town of Council Bluffs, Iowa, to pick up the money. David McCanles sent his twelve-year-old son, Monroe, to make the trip with Wellman.

Upon Wellman's return ten days later, David McCanles, accompanied by two friends, went to the station once more to obtain his payment and to reunite with his son Monroe. Mrs. Wellman told McCanles that her husband could not come out to speak with him. McCanles grew angry and told Mrs. Wellman that if her husband would not come out, then he would go in and drag him out. At this point Hickok suddenly appeared in the doorway. McCanles was somewhat bewildered by Hickok's interest in the argument and asked Hickok for a drink of water in order to buy time. After drinking, McCanles circled the cabin and entered the back door while Hickok hid behind a curtain that separated the two rooms of the cabin. McCanles called to Hickok to come out and fight fair. Hickok responded by firing a single shot from behind the curtain, piercing McCanles's heart.

The two men who had arrived with McCanles heard the shot and ran toward the cabin. Hickok appeared in the doorway and fired four shots from his revolver, wounding both men. One man ran around the side of the cabin followed by Wellman, who had suddenly appeared with a hoe, screaming "Let's kill them all."[8] The other man fled toward the creek. Wellman killed the man by crushing his skull with the hoe and then attempted to kill McCanles's son, who was kneeling over his slain father. The terrified youth ran and managed to elude his pursuers by escaping into the brush. Wellman and Hickok followed the trail of blood left by the second man, found him, and then one of them killed him with a blast from a shotgun, thus completing the triple murder.

As a result of the questionable circumstances of the fight, Hickok and Wellman were charged with murder. The trial took place in the log cabin of "Pap" Towle, the local justice of the peace. The defendants claimed self-defense; Monroe McCanles, the son of David McCanles, despite having witnessed the gunfight and having to flee for his life, was not allowed to testify and was even banned from the "courtroom" during the testimonies of Hickok and Wellman. Wellman and Hickok, employees of the Overland Stage Company, the most powerful corporation west of Missouri, were found innocent by a jury composed of the company's line drivers and stable hands.

Hickok in the Civil War

Shortly after the McCanles murder trial, the Civil War broke out, and Hickok signed up to serve the Union army as a civilian scout.

Hickok was an employee of the Overland Stage Company, the most powerful corporation in the West.

Official documents reveal that Hickok took part in the Battle of Wilson's Creek in August 1861, during which Union general Nathaniel Lyon was killed and his soldiers were forced to flee before the Confederate army. Hickok escaped with his life and turned up later that fall working as a wagon master for the Union forces.

By 1864, Hickok was again working as a scout for the Union army, spying on enemy troop movements in southern Missouri. On June 9, 1865, Hickok was discharged from the army and drifted to Springfield, Missouri.

It was during the Civil War that Hickok earned the nickname "Wild Bill," supposedly for his reckless charges across enemy lines and for wild gun battles on horseback. However, it is more likely that Hickok earned the nickname while protecting a bartender friend who had killed a drunken teamster in Independence, Missouri. When a crowd gathered in front of the saloon where the killing took place, demanding revenge for their friend's death, Hickok reportedly drew his revolver, pointed it at the crowd, and warned, "Leave or there will be more dead men around here than the town can bury." The crowd wavered; they had heard the story of Rock Creek. After a few jeers and curses, the crowd dispersed. A woman who had been watching called out, "Good for you, Wild Bill,"[9] and the name stuck.

Hickok's Gunfight with Dave Tutt

In postwar Springfield, Missouri, Hickock pursued the two activities that would come to dominate his life: drinking and gambling.

It was here that he became friends with a man named Dave Tutt, an Arkansas gambler. Their friendship soon dissolved, however, in a quarrel over a game of cards, which escalated when they disagreed about the amount of money Hickok owed Tutt for an old debt. Tutt snatched Hickok's watch from the gaming table and told Hickok that he planned to wear it the next day on the market square. Hickok told Tutt that, if he did, Tutt would pay with his life.

The gunfight between Hickok and Tutt took place on the morning of July 21, 1865. It is one of the few examples of the "stand-up" gunfight popularized by Hollywood and western novels. At 6:00 A.M. both men appeared at opposite ends of the town square and began to slowly advance toward each other while the townspeople, who had risen early for the event, watched. When the men were about seventy-five yards apart, Hickok warned Tutt to stop. Tutt kept moving toward Hickok, pulled his six-gun, and fired a shot, but it missed. Hickok then drew his own weapon with his right hand, steadied it with his left hand, and squeezed off a single round that struck Tutt in the heart, killing him instantly. Hickok turned his guns over to the sheriff and was arrested on a charge of murder.

Hickok's trial was short, and he was acquitted on the grounds that he had acted in self-defense. The verdict upset many people in Springfield. Despite the scorn of the citizens, Hickok remained in town and even campaigned for the post of town marshal. The voters made their feelings about Hickok clear: He lost the election.

Hickok's Cavalry Career

After his unsuccessful run for office, Hickok moved west and returned to his previous line of work, this time as a civilian scout for the U.S. cavalry under the command of General George Armstrong Custer. General Custer had only praise for Hickok:

> Whether on foot or on horseback he was one of the most perfect types of physical manhood I ever saw. Of his courage there could be no question: it has been brought to the test on too many occasions to doubt. His skill in the use of the rifle and pistol was unerring. . . . Wild Bill is anything but a quarrelsome man; yet no one but himself can enumerate the many conflicts in which he has engaged, and which have almost invariably resulted in the death of his adversary. I have personal knowledge of at least half a dozen men whom he has at various times

killed, one of these being a member of my command. Others have been severely wounded, yet he always escaped unhurt.[10]

Hickok was also physically impressive. General Custer's wife was particularly taken with him:

Physically he was a delight to look upon. Tall, lithe and free in every motion, he made and walked as if every muscle was perfection, and the careless swing of his body as he moved seemed perfectly in keeping with the man, the country, the time in which he lived. I do not recall anything finer in the way of physical perfection than Wild Bill when he swung himself lightly from his saddle, and with graceful, swaying steps, squarely set shoulders and well pointed head, approached our tent for orders. . . . He did not make an armoury of his waist, but carried two pistols. . . . I do not remember his features but the frankly, manly expression of his fearless eyes and his courteous manner gave one a feeling of confidence in his word and his undaunted courage.[11]

James Hickok worked as a member of the U.S. Cavalry where a wound inflicted upon his thigh by a Cheyenne Indian ended his army career.

Hickok's duties as a civilian scout were dangerous. During the winter of 1869, while delivering dispatches between Fort Lyon and Fort Wallace, Hickok was attacked by a Cheyenne war party. In a running fight he was wounded in the thigh by an Indian lance but managed to escape. Hickok's wound, inflicted by a broad-bladed spearhead, was slow to heal. After weeks in the army hospital, he decided to return home to La Salle County to recuperate. Hickok's army career was at an end, but he would not be satisfied with retirement for long.

Hickok quickly grew bored with life on the farm and traveled north to Chicago, where he visited his boyhood friend Herman

Baldwin. The two men were playing billiards when they were accosted by several toughs who made fun of Hickok's long hair and buckskin clothing. A fight ensued, and Hickok beat the men into unconsciousness with a pool cue.

A short time later, Hickok left Illinois to guide Senator Henry S. Wilson and a party of politicians on a five-week tour of the plains. The senator rewarded Hickok by paying him $500 and giving him two ivory-handled custom-made Colt revolvers, which Hickok wore for the rest of his life. Once the tour ended, the senator returned to Washington, D.C., and Hickok wandered into Kansas, where his growing reputation gained him his next job.

Hickok's Law Enforcement Career

In August 1869, Hickok was appointed sheriff of Ellis County, Kansas, which included Hays City, a rough-and-tumble frontier town. From the beginning, Hickok made it known that he intended to keep the peace. With his twin ivory-handled Colts at his hip, a knife in his boot, and a shotgun cradled in his arms, Hickok impressed even the rowdiest of citizens. However, there were those in the town who thought they could enhance their own reputation by killing Hickok. One of these was a man named Sullivan who got the "drop" on Hickok. Sullivan held a pistol to Hickok's head and called to passersby to watch as he dispatched the sheriff. While Sullivan talked, Hickok's hand inched toward his holster. He drew his own gun suddenly and killed Sullivan with one shot. Hickok's comment on the incident was brief: "He talked his life away."[12]

Despite the fact that the killing was clearly in self-defense, the townspeople felt a sense of dissatisfaction with their lawman, and in 1870 Hickok was voted out of office. He left town without incident but returned in July of the same year to experience one of his narrowest scrapes. Hickok was drinking in a saloon when he was attacked by two troopers from his old army outfit, the Seventh Cavalry. What caused the fight is unknown, but the result was all too clear: Hickok killed one trooper and wounded the other. Hickok fled Hays City just ahead of a cavalry detachment with orders to take him dead or alive. The detachment chased Hickok across Kansas and Missouri to St. Louis, where he found refuge with influential friends who were members of the Missouri state legislature.

Hickok in Abilene, Kansas

Despite having been chased out of Kansas, Hickok returned to the state, and in 1871, he was appointed marshal of Abilene, Kansas.

Hickok would have his skills as a gunfighter put to the test. For six months of the year, Abilene was just another sleepy frontier town composed primarily of farmers and merchants, but for the other six months of the year, it was a raucous place where cowboys would ride their horses up and down the main street "hurrahing" the town—firing their pistols into the air and at anything that took their fancy. Violence was common and death was a frequent visitor. The dawn of each day would often find a new corpse in the dusty streets. The cowboys were quick-draw artists who would do as they were told when sober, but when intoxicated, they proved to be belligerent and uncontrollable. The citizens of Abilene hoped that Hickok's reputation as a killer would prove to be an asset and not a liability.

Hickok replaced the town's former marshal, Tom Smith, who had been killed in the line of duty. After Hickok was appointed marshal, he wasted no time in cleaning up the town. He convinced the city council to pass an ordinance against carrying firearms within the city limits. On June 8, 1871, an editorial in the *Abilene Chronicle* made it clear that the citizens of Abilene were behind their new marshal:

> Fire Arms—The Chief of Police [James B. Hickok] has posted notices, informing all persons that the ordinance against carrying fire arms or other weapons in Abilene, will be enforced. That's right. There's no bravery in carrying revolvers in a civilized community. Such a practice is well enough and perhaps necessary when among Indians, . . . but among white people it ought to be discountenanced.[13]

Although some cowboys chose to ignore the ordinance, it did result in fewer gunfights in town during the eight months that Hickok served as marshal.

Hickok made the Alamo Saloon his headquarters and patrolled Abilene's dusty streets with his ivory-handled Colts holstered and at the ready, a large knife in his belt, two derringers hidden in the pockets of his frock coat, and a shotgun or rifle cradled in one arm. The sight of the heavily armed marshal was enough to intimidate all but the most drunken cowboys. As one Texas cowboy later recalled,

> When I came along the street, he was standing there with his back to the wall and his thumbs hooked in his red sash. He stood there and rolled his head from side to side looking at everything and everybody from under his eye-

brows—just like a mad old bull. I decided then and there I didn't want any part of him.[14]

When Hickok wasn't busy controlling the cowboys or drinking and gambling in the Alamo, he would shoot stray dogs and clear the street of the dead animals. Hickok also cleaned up Abilene in other ways. He arrested vagrants, closed down illicit gambling games, and supervised the removal of the dance halls and brothels from Abilene's main thoroughfare, Texas Street. In one famous incident he forced the owners of the Bull Head Saloon—at gunpoint—to paint over the pornographic sign in front of their business. Hickok's action caused hard feelings between him and the owners, Ben Thompson (a well-respected gunfighter in his own right) and Phil Coe. Hickok would see more of Coe in the future.

During his stint as marshal of Abilene, Hickok met many of the most famous gunfighters and outlaws of the era, and he wisely avoided confrontation. For example, when Frank and Jesse James slipped into Abilene while on the run from the law, they passed word to Hickok that they would make no trouble while in town, but added that they had arranged for his funeral in the event that he tried to arrest them.

Hickok's "live and let live" philosophy also worked to his advantage in dealing with fellow gunman John Wesley Hardin. After Hickok and Hardin shared a couple of drinks, the two men came to an agreement. Hardin would be allowed to keep his guns for protection, but if he killed anyone, Hickok would kill him. At one point, Hardin was approached by fellow Texan Ben Thompson, who offered to pay Hardin to kill Hickok. Hardin declined, saying that Hickok was an honorable man and that if Thompson wanted Hickok dead, he should do it himself.

Jesse James was another well-known gunfighter who Hickok wisely avoided. Here, Jesse James is pictured on the cover of a newspaper.

Hickok's Last Gunfight

While Hickok was marshal of Abilene, he enforced the law without resorting to his guns, until the night of October 5, 1871, when a band of drunken cowboys was wandering the streets, firing their guns into the air and demanding that passersby buy them drinks. When Hickok heard a shot fired outside the Alamo Saloon, he hurried outside to find out who had fired it. In the street, he confronted Phil Coe, pistol in hand, and the band of drunken cowboys. Coe claimed he had been shooting at a stray dog. During the brief argument that ensued, Coe pulled a second pistol, which prompted Hickok to pull his own pistols. Coe fired first. His first shot went through Hickok's coattail and his second shot struck the ground between Hickok's legs. Hickok fired next, both of his bullets striking Coe in the stomach. The fatally wounded man collapsed into the dust.

But the violence was not over. From the corner of his eye, Hickok saw a figure from the shadows rushing at him with a gun in his hand. Believing that his life was in danger, he fired twice at the shadowy figure. When the smoke cleared, Hickok realized the mistake he had made. The unknown gunman turned out to be Hickok's personal friend and onetime deputy Michael Williams, who had been rushing to help Hickok. Visibly shaken after realizing what had happened, Hickok picked up his dead friend, took him inside the Alamo, and laid him on a billiards table. He then went back outside and dispersed the mob of cowboys with threats and curses.

The fight with Coe and the killing of Williams had a great effect on Hickok. Although sentiment in the town was generally with Hickok, the town council refused to renew his contract. He was dismissed as marshal on December 13, 1871. Leaving his post as marshal did not mean that Hickok was in the clear, however. Coe's friends began to make threats against Hickok's life, so Hickok began to carry a sawed-off shotgun under his coat as protection in case of ambush. Indeed, on a train ride from Abilene to Topeka, an attempt was made on Hickok's life by five cowboys determined to avenge Coe's death. Hickok managed to circumvent the ambush and forced the Texans at gunpoint to remain on the train while he got off in Topeka.

Hickok's Later Years

For the next two years Hickok drifted across the West. Jobless and unsteady with drink, Hickok wandered from town to town playing cards and occasionally serving as a tour guide for groups of wealthy Easterners who were willing to pay to be shown something of the Wild West.

The West's wildness was quickly vanishing, but some tried to preserve it in the form of traveling shows. In 1873, his old friend William "Buffalo Bill" Cody invited Hickok to tour the East Coast with him and act in Cody's melodrama *The Scouts of the Plains*. The relationship was a disaster. Hickok was often drunk during performances and unable to remember his lines. He also had a high voice that was hard for audiences to hear. Hickok wanted to be the star, and he threatened to kill the stagehands unless they kept the spotlight on him. Cody eventually had to fire Hickok after he shot blanks at the bare legs of the actors dressed up as Native Americans to make them jump and howl like "good Injun[s]."[15]

With the failure of his stage career, Hickok returned to the West and resumed wandering from town to town, gambling and drinking heavily, but he was a pale shadow of his former self. He was arrested for vagrancy several times. To make matters worse, his eyesight began to fail, which hindered his once deadly marksmanship. Deprived of this asset, Hickok found his life increasingly at risk. During his lifetime, Hickok had made many enemies, and many others sought to enhance their own reputation by killing the famous gunfighter. Wherever he went, Hickok made certain to keep his back to the wall and an eye on his surroundings.

In his later life, James Hickok was repeatedly attacked by the many enemies he had formed in his youthful days of gunfighting.

A Little Peace

By early 1876, Hickok had found some measure of peace and established himself in Cheyenne, Wyoming, where he worked as a hunting guide for tourists from the East Coast and Europe. It was in Cheyenne that Hickok resumed a love affair with Agnes Lake Thatcher, a circus owner and performer he had met in Abilene in 1871. Hickok and Thatcher were married in Cheyenne on March

5, 1876, and following a honeymoon in St. Louis, Missouri, the newlyweds returned to Cheyenne in the late spring. Hickok, however, unable to stay in one place for long and needing money, soon left for the Black Hills of the Dakota Territory to prospect for gold.

Hickok made the town of Deadwood in the Dakota Territory his base of operations and by most accounts avoided trouble while in town, preferring to prospect for gold alone and occasionally play a quiet game of poker. Hickok wrote to his wife in Cheyenne on a regular basis and expressed his desire to be reunited with her as soon as possible.

Hickok stayed out of trouble until the night of August 1, 1876, when he played cards with John "Jack" McCall, a small cross-eyed man. In the card game, Hickok cleaned out McCall. When McCall complained that he had no money for breakfast, Hickok gave him some money and advised him not to gamble unless he could afford to lose.

A Fatal Card Game

The next afternoon, August 2, Hickok was playing cards with three other men in Saloon Number 10. Hickok was uneasy while he played because his back was toward the saloon's two open doors. He asked each of the men to trade seats with him but was refused by each in turn because they too were afraid of being shot in the back. At about 4:00 P.M. McCall entered the saloon without Hickok's noticing, ordered a drink at the bar, drank it, walked up behind Hickok, pulled out an old six-gun, and fired it once into the back of Hickok's head. The great gunman fell sideways out of his chair to the floor still clutching his poker hand, aces and eights. A poker hand with that combination of cards would be known from then on as the "deadman's hand."

McCall fled the saloon but was captured in a nearby barbershop and charged with murder. In his trial, McCall was acquitted on the grounds of self-defense, but that trial was later ruled illegal by the territorial court. McCall was tried a second time and this time was found guilty of murder. McCall was executed on March 1, 1877. In a final bit of irony, when asked why he did not challenge Hickok face-to-face, McCall responded that to do so would have been suicidal.

The obituaries that appeared after Hickok's death generally lauded the man and criticized his murderer. For example, the *Ellis County Star*, published in Hays City, where Hickok had once served as marshal, noted:

While here he killed several men; but all their acquaintances agreed that he was justified in so doing. He never provoked a quarrel, and was a generous, gentlemanly fellow. . . . Had the fellow that shot him given him a fair fight, and not taken the cowardly advantage that he did, Wild Bill would not have been killed.[16]

Hickok was buried in a cemetery on the south side of Deadwood on August 3, 1876. His body was later exhumed and moved to a new location on Mount Moriah, on the other side of Deadwood, where an elaborate memorial was erected in his honor.

CHAPTER 3

The Gunfighter's Gunfighter: Ben Thompson

Jolly, well mannered, and distinctive in his silk stovepipe hat, tailored suits, and carefully waxed mustache, Ben Thompson cut a wide and lethal path across the West. Few men could have crowded more drama into a forty-one-year life span than Ben Thompson did. He was by turns a Confederate cavalry officer, a mercenary, an Indian fighter, a gambler, a businessman, a lawman, and, above all, a precise and ruthless gunfighter.

The exact date and location of Ben Thompson's birth are unknown. He was born in either Canada or England in about 1843. What is known is that his parents were English and that his father worked as a sailor. The Thompson family moved to Austin, Texas, when Ben was nine years old, and he soon had to learn to be tough. By the time he was twelve, Ben and his younger brother, Billy, were fighting daily battles with the bullies who tormented their father as he staggered his way home from the saloons where he spent the majority of his time.

People who knew Ben as a boy recalled that he was "bright, handsome, full of promise and owning an explosive temper."[17] This temper manifested itself at the age of thirteen when Thompson shot another boy in a dispute over marksmanship. (The boy lived to pick the bird shot out of his skin.)

By this time, Ben's father had abandoned the family, and Ben and Billy Thompson were left to support their mother and two sisters. Ben Thompson attracted the attention of Colonel John A. Green, a prominent Austin lawyer who was impressed by Thompson's intelligence and thought the young man had potential. Colonel Green paid for Thompson to attend a private school, but, although he proved to be a bright pupil, he was forced to return home after two years in order to work to support his mother.

Colonel Green again came to Thompson's rescue, this time getting him a job in the composing room of Austin's *Southern Intelligencer*. Thompson did well at the paper and soon became an apprentice printer. He stayed only a year, however, and then moved to New Orleans, Louisiana, where he found work as a printer on the *New Orleans Picayune*.

Thompson's stay in New Orleans was soon cut short. One day while riding a horse car (a form of public transportation) through New Orleans, Thompson noticed a young Frenchman, Emile de Tour, forcing his attentions on a young woman. Thompson inter-

Although Ben Thompson's life started out with a private education and good job, his first duel in New Orleans gave him a reputation as a formidable gunfighter.

vened, and in the ensuing fight, he threw de Tour off the horse car. Humiliated, de Tour traced Thompson to the *Picayune* office and challenged him to a duel with pistols or swords. But since Thompson was the challenged party, he had the right to choose his weapons under the *code duello* (dueling code) observed by the city's residents. The Texan shocked the Frenchman by insisting that they enter a darkened room blindfolded and fight to the death with knives. After some argument, de Tour agreed.

The following day at dawn, de Tour and Thompson were blindfolded, given Bowie knives, and guided into an abandoned icehouse on the outskirts of New Orleans. The door to the icehouse was then locked from the outside. The second for each man waited outside. After a few minutes, there was a knock, and they rushed to open the door. Thompson, still blindfolded, stepped out. Behind him on the floor was de Tour's lifeless body. That night, de Tour's friends scoured the city for Thompson, but on the advice of friends who feared for his life, Thompson had already left New Orleans for Austin.

The Beginning of Thompson's Career as a Gunfighter and a Gambler

Upon his return to Austin, Thompson returned to work as a printer for the *Intelligencer*. His free time he spent gambling. Thompson discovered that he was skilled not only as a gambler but as a marksman. Skill at cards and gunplay looked to be a winning combination, so Thompson quit the newspaper and became a full-time gambler. Gambling, though, would not be the way Thompson would make his reputation.

Austin in the mid–nineteenth century was still a frontier settlement subject to raids by Native Americans. When a war party of Comanche and Kiowa swept through Austin and kidnapped five girls, Thompson joined the posse that caught the kidnappers. In the gunfight that ensued, Thompson killed all the members of the war party except one. The girls were rescued, and with this feat Thompson's reputation as a marksman was firmly established. That marksmanship soon came in handy.

Thompson in the Civil War

In 1861, when the Civil War broke out, Thompson joined the Confederate army, enlisting in the Second Cavalry. His first fight, however, was not against the Yankees. Soon after enlisting, Thompson brawled with a lieutenant and a sergeant and killed them both. Following the fight, Thompson was jailed, but he managed to escape. In the confusion caused by the war, he was able to join a different cavalry outfit.

During the war, Thompson was involved in several battles, including the Battle of LaFourche Crossing in 1863, in which his regiment was decimated. It was while he was on leave after this battle that Thompson returned to Austin and married Catherine "Kate" Moore, the daughter of a local farmer. Thompson returned to duty, however, this time as a lieutenant attached to Colonel John Ford's regiment, which was patrolling along the Rio Grande. Again, much of the action Thompson saw did not involve enemy troops.

Lieutenant Thompson divided his time with Ford's regiment soldiering, gambling, and smuggling whiskey across the Mexican border. Gambling and guns proved to be a lethal combination when Thompson was around. In Laredo, Texas, Thompson killed two Mexicans in a gambling hall dispute and fled back to Austin just ahead of a posse that gave up the pursuit because their horses were exhausted. A short time after his arrival in Austin, Thompson was again involved in a gambling dispute, this time with a man named John Coombs. In the ensuing fight, Thompson killed Coombs and as a result was arrested and charged with murder. Again, Thompson managed to escape and rejoined the Confederate army, where he served until General Lee's surrender on April 9, 1865.

Thompson After the Civil War

With the end of the Civil War, Thompson returned to Austin to be reunited with his wife (who had just given birth to his son) and his brother, Billy. There was little time to enjoy his family, however. A few days later, both Thompsons were arrested and charged with the Coombs killing. Texas at this time was operating under martial law, which meant that few protections existed for those charged with crimes. Like many prisoners in postwar Texas, the two brothers languished in prison for several months without a hearing and without lawyers, and their appeals for release on bail were denied.

Meanwhile, in Mexico, Emperor Maximilian was struggling to hold on to his throne and dispatching agents to recruit former Confederate officers to help him. Mexican agents contacted Ben Thompson in prison and offered him a lieutenant's commission in the emperor's army. Thompson accepted and, bribed by the Mexican agents, his guards let Thompson slip out of prison one night. Thompson crossed the Rio Grande into Matamoros, Mexico, where he joined the regiment of General Tomas Mejia.

Thompson saw a lot of combat in Mexico. In one of the battles he fought, more than three-quarters of his force was destroyed. Eventually, Maximilian was defeated, and with no official protection, Thompson fled Mexico. Mistakenly believing that martial law had ended in Texas, Thompson returned to Austin, where he was arrested on the outstanding murder charge. At the conclusion of a five-week trial, Thompson was found guilty and sentenced to ten years' hard labor in the prison in Huntsville, Texas.

Thompson in Abilene, Kansas

Fortunately for Thompson, two years later Texas returned to civilian rule, and he was released from prison. Thompson resumed the life of a gambler and drifted through several Texas towns plying his trade. Cowboys returning from cattle drives told Thompson that Abilene, Kansas, was wide open and a gambler's paradise. The year was 1870; Thompson decided to try his luck in Abilene.

Leaving his wife in Austin, Thompson rode north and arrived in Abilene, Kansas, in June 1871 with just enough money to buy a night's lodging and breakfast. Thompson pawned his six-shooter and sat in on the first poker game he could find. When the game ended several hours later, Thompson was richer by $2,583.

Phil Coe, another Austin gambler who had served with Thompson during the Civil War, arrived in Abilene at about the same time. The two men renewed their friendship. Together, they opened the Bull Head Saloon, which soon became the most notorious gambling house and saloon in Abilene's rowdy history. The Bull Head was a booming success and became the favorite haunt of the thousands of cowboys who came to Abilene.

However, the saloon was not without controversy. Shortly after the business opened, city officials demanded that Coe and Thompson change the Bull Head sign, an exaggerated (and according to the officials, pornographic) painting of a longhorn's sexual organ. When Coe and Thompson ignored the complaint, the town marshal, Wild Bill Hickok, marched to the saloon and forced them at gunpoint to paint over the sign. Hickok also forced Coe and Thompson to move their faro equipment out of the back room and into the front of the establishment. These confrontations soured relations between Coe, Thompson, and Hickok.

From their first meeting, Thompson and Hickok had viewed each other with hostility and suspicion. Thompson hated all Yankees but especially former Union soldiers. Hickok was equally contemptuous of Southerners, especially Texans. Although Hickok and Thompson never had a fight, tensions between the two men grew. When John Wesley Hardin, another gunman whose reputation as a killer preceded him, arrived in Abilene, Thompson offered to pay him to kill Hickok. Hardin declined, however, saying that if Thompson wanted Hickok dead, he should do it himself.

By midsummer 1871, Abilene had quieted down and Thompson, lonely for his family, telegraphed his wife to join him in Kansas. Kate and Thompson's six-year-old son arrived in Kansas City, Missouri, a short time later and the family was reunited. However, the happiness was short-lived. While taking a ride around the city, the carriage the Thompsons were riding in over-

Hickok's reputation was viewed with hostility and suspicion by Thompson and other well-known gunfighters.

turned, severely injuring all three. Kate suffered a crushed arm, which had to be amputated; their son broke his foot; and Ben fractured his leg. Doctors treated the family for the rest of the summer and into the fall at the Lincoln Hotel in Kansas City. While recovering, Thompson decided that he had seen enough of Kansas and it was time to return to Texas.

Thompson and Coe sold the Bull Head in September 1871, and the Thompsons slowly moved back to Texas by rail and stagecoach while Coe remained behind to work as a professional gambler. Bad news caught up with Thompson, however. Somewhere between Abilene and Austin, Thompson met Bud Cotton, a fellow Texan, accompanying Phil Coe's casket. Cotton told Thompson how Coe had died in a gunfight with Hickok. Cotton concluded by telling Thompson, "There was only one man who could have faced him—and you weren't there, Ben."[18] The news grieved Thompson; Cotton later recalled that the gunfighter put his head on Coe's casket and wept.

Thompson in Ellsworth, Kansas

For months after returning to Austin, Thompson was moody and irritable. Coe's death and the injuries to his wife and son had changed him. He avoided saloons and gambling halls and flatly refused to take part in big stakes card games. It took Thompson more than a year to come to grips with the death of his friend and the misfortune that had struck his own family. Eventually, though, tales he heard attracted his interest. Ellsworth, Kansas, cowboys said, was a cow town that was twice as big and open as Abilene. Ben decided to try his luck in Ellsworth and took his brother, Billy, with him.

Ben and Billy Thompson arrived in Ellsworth in June 1873 and opened a gambling house in the rear of a saloon. Ben Thompson was popular with the cowhands, and his "gambler's roost" was soon a success. Despite the stories that Thompson had heard in Austin, however, Ellsworth was not as wild as Abilene. Cowboys fresh from the trail would ride into town shooting at signs and shattering windows and street lamps, but there were few gunfights. The sheriff of Ellsworth, Chauncy B. Whitney, allowed the drovers to blow off steam and then made them pay for the damages, usually buying them a drink afterward. Ben Thompson and Whitney soon became friends, and Thompson would occasionally help Whitney disarm a drunken cowhand.

Things went well until the afternoon of August 15, 1873. Early in the afternoon, Thompson confronted another gambler, Jack

Chauncy Whitney, the sheriff of Ellsworth County, was shot and killed by Ben Thompson's brother, Billy Thompson.

Sterling, over money Sterling owed him. Sterling started a fistfight with Thompson, but two deputies, "Happy Jack" Morco and Edward Hogue, broke up the altercation.

Later that afternoon, Ben and Billy Thompson, now armed, went looking for Sterling and Morco. Billy Thompson, who had been drinking all afternoon, was drunk by the time he joined his brother. The two brothers confronted Sterling and Morco by the railroad depot, and Ben Thompson offered Sterling and Morco a chance to fight. Sheriff Whitney, who had been summoned, tried to act as peacemaker. Unarmed, he walked toward the Thompsons and asked the brothers to end the confrontation. Ben Thompson agreed on the condition that he and Billy would be under Whitney's protection.

What happened next was retold by Thompson at his trial:

> We started to the Grand Central Hotel, he [Whitney] and Billy walking in advance, I in the rear. I kept a vigilant watch in every direction, believing as I did, that either of the two men I have named [Sterling and Morco] would not hesitate to assassinate me, although in the hands, or rather in charge of the Sheriff. Glancing behind me when near the hotel, I saw Happy Jack, about sixty yards away, come around the corner of a store, gun in hand. . . . I right-about faced instantly, and drew my gun down on him and fired; but he dodged behind the corner from which he had come too quick for me. This conduct on his part enraged me, and I concluded to have it out with him then and there, and for that reason started in a rapid walk toward him. The shooting drew the attention of the Sheriff and Billy, the latter of whom [Billy Thompson] stopped, while the other [Sheriff Whitney] started toward me. . . . I heard the report of a gun behind me, and, turning, found that Sher-

iff Whitney had been shot. I ran to him, all thought of Happy Jack leaping out of my mind. I also saw Billy lowering his gun; I exclaimed, "My God, Billy, what have you done; you have shot our best friend[!]"[19]

Drawn by the sound of gunfire, a mob formed and surrounded the Thompson brothers and the dying sheriff. Ben, fearing for his brother's life, gave Billy one of his guns and some money and urged his sibling to flee. Billy fled to a cow camp on the edge of town. Ben Thompson stayed to face the angry crowd alone. Thompson held the mob at bay until the mayor arrived, and then he surrendered. Ben and Billy Thompson were charged with murder, but Sheriff Whitney's deathbed testimony that the shooting was accidental helped win their acquittal.

Thompson left Ellsworth and wandered about Texas and the West gambling in various boomtowns that seemed to die almost as suddenly as they were born. Eventually, in 1876, Thompson went to work for the Atchison, Topeka, and Santa Fe Railroad as a hired gun. Thompson was well paid for his services: $2,300 and several diamonds. With his payment in hand, Thompson returned to Austin, where he opened yet another gambling hall and saloon.

Thompson's Law Enforcement Career

Ben Thompson appeared to have achieved some peace, but by the late 1870s, his reputation as a gunfighter had reached New York City and attracted the attention of its newspapers. The editor of the *New York Sun* sent a reporter to Texas to interview Thompson, and his answer to a question about his gunfighting strategy suggests something of his character:

> I always make it a rule to let the other fellow fire first. If a man wants to fight, I always argue the question with him and try to show him how foolish it would be. If he can't be dissuaded, why, then the fun begins but I always let him have first crack. Then when I fire, you see, I have the verdict of self-defense on

Billy Thompson led a similar lifestyle to that of his brother Ben. Billy and Ben opened a gambling house together in 1873 in the town of Ellsworth.

39

my side. I know that he is pretty certain in his hurry, to miss. I never do.[20]

By the end of the 1870s, Thompson was a respected citizen of Austin, and in 1879 he decided to run for the public office of city marshal of Austin, Texas. His campaign was based on the notion that he was an honest defender of his fellow citizens. He challenged anyone to prove that he had ever been dishonest or had ignored the cries "of the defenseless, timid and weak to protect them from the aggressions and wrongs of the over bearing and strong."[21] The Robin Hood image failed to sway a majority of Austin voters, however, and Thompson was defeated. But the following year Thompson ran for the office again, and won by more than two hundred votes.

Ben Thompson proved to be a superb law enforcement officer. From the moment he took office, the crime rate in Austin dropped. Public records reveal that not a single murder or burglary occurred within the town's limits during his time in office. His appearance on the street was enough to keep things peaceful, and he treated everyone, regardless of race, alike. Thompson was such an effective lawman that the citizens forgave his shortcomings, such as getting drunk and shooting out street lamps when things got too quiet.

Thompson's law enforcement career might have continued indefinitely had it not been for a confrontation he had in the summer of 1882 in San Antonio, Texas. Thompson took his diamonds (the ones he had received as part of his payment for his work with the Atchison, Topeka, and Santa Fe Railroad) to Jack Harris, the owner of San Antonio's Vaudeville Theater, for an appraisal, since Harris worked part-time as a jeweler. The two men argued over the value of the gems. Thompson left but returned on July 11, 1882, with his gun. Harris, hearing that Thompson was gunning for him, armed himself with a double-barrel shotgun and waited for Thompson at the theater. Thompson approached the theater near sunset, peered through the windows, and saw Harris, inside, cradling his shotgun. There was an exchange of profanity, Harris raised the shotgun to fire, and Thompson, always quick on the draw, got off the first shot and then fired two more into Harris as the dying man attempted to pull the trigger of his shotgun.

Thompson was arrested, charged with murder, and released on bail. He was forced to resign as marshal of Austin and stand trial in San Antonio for the murder of Harris. Thompson's murder trial attracted wide attention. Huge crowds flocked to the courthouse to catch a glimpse of the famous gunfighter. The prosecutor tried to prove that Thompson had provoked the fight, but eyewitnesses testified that he was only defending himself. The jury deliberated for a few hours before acquitting him.

Thompson received a hero's welcome when he returned to Austin. He was greeted by a brass band, city officials, and prominent merchants. Men and women waved hats and handkerchiefs from windows and rooftops greeting the famous gunfighter. However, Thompson found that business was bad at his gambling house; he had to close early some days for lack of customers. Thompson would sit in the darkened bar alone, drinking and brooding.

Thompson's Later Years

Thompson began to suffer from insomnia, and he would prowl the deserted streets of Austin at night shooting at signs and streetlights (the police always found it convenient to be elsewhere). His behavior became more and more erratic. For example, one day he shattered an Italian organ grinder's organ with gunfire only to find the terrified man later and pay him for the damages. Sometimes he would visit the composing rooms of the *Daily Austin Statesman* and reminisce about his days as a printer on the *Austin Intelligencer;* other times he would enter the composing room roaring drunk, kick over the boxes of type, and send the printers fleeing from his gunfire. On one occasion he barged into the annual dinner of the Cattlemans' Convention flourishing his guns, using the water pitchers as targets and sending the cattlemen running for their lives. The newspapers and the citizens began to turn against him. One newspaper editorialized, "He is a curse to Texas . . . what kind of meat is he eating?"[22]

A Violent End

Thompson lived by the gun and died by the gun. On March 11, 1884, Thompson met up with J. King Fisher, a gunfighter and sometime lawman and rustler, who was in Austin on business. The two men began a tour of the city's saloons and drank all day, with Thompson's mood getting uglier and uglier. As the day waned, Fisher talked Thompson into going to San Antonio for more merriment.

The two men arrived in San Antonio at about 8:00 P.M. They caught a play at Turner's Hall, and then Fisher convinced Thompson to go to the Vaudeville Theater, where Thompson had killed Jack Harris two years earlier. Thompson had vowed never to step foot in the place again because "it would be my graveyard,"[23] but he went anyway.

Fisher and Thompson entered the Vaudeville Theater and were greeted by Billy Simms, a childhood friend of Thompson's, and joined by Jacob S. Coy, a San Antonio policeman. The four men sat at a table and began drinking. Thompson then demanded to see Joe Foster, who had been Jack Harris's partner. Foster appeared but refused to shake Thompson's hand or accept his offer of a drink. The events that followed put an end to Thompson's violent life:

> Thompson and Fisher sprang up . . . [but] before they got to their feet a volley sounded as though there was a dozen carbines, was fired from a box [balcony] that was a little to the left and considerably above the doomed men and both went down instantly. . . . Thompson fell on his right side and as he did so, Simms or Coy rushed by and drew his revolver and bent over, putting the muzzle close to his [Thompson's] ear and fired. He then fired other shots into his [Thompson's] head and body and the other man shot Fisher in a similar manner.[24]

An investigation revealed that Thompson and Fisher had been killed by three concealed gunmen armed with Winchester rifles. Neither Coy, Foster, nor Simms was ever charged with murder, even though popular opinion was that they had conspired to kill Thompson. Fisher's role in the shooting is still something of a mystery. The question remains whether he was actually friends with Thompson or merely a decoy who had been double-crossed by his coconspirators.

In Austin, Ben Thompson's friends and admirers gave him a monumental funeral. The church overflowed with people, and the line of mourners stretched for blocks. One of the many carriages was filled with weeping orphans. It was only at the funeral that people learned that Ben Thompson, the gambler and gunfighter, had been providing the orphans with clothing and food for years.

CHAPTER 4

Hollywood's Favorite Lawman: Wyatt Berry Stapp Earp

Although many died a violent death, some gunfighters actually managed to die of old age. Wyatt Earp's name is synonymous with the Hollywood image of the gunfighter who upheld the law. Indeed, more movies and television shows have been made about the life of Wyatt Earp than perhaps that of any other western gunfighter. The truth is that Earp rarely fired his weapon in the course of his law enforcement duties and instead often beat lawbreakers into submission. Wyatt Earp's reputation rests primarily on one incident, the shootout at the O.K. Corral. Although Earp was a reluctant gunfighter, his participation in the shootout at the O.K. Corral has given him the status of mythic hero in the popular imagination.

Wyatt Berry Stapp Earp was born on March 19, 1848, the fourth of seven children. His father, Nicholas Earp, named Wyatt after the officer he served under during the Mexican-American War, Colonel Wyatt Berry Stapp. Wyatt and all of his siblings were born in Kentucky, but early on the family moved to Iowa, where they worked a large farm. Some years later, the Earps moved on to California, settling near San Bernardino.

The Earp boys—James, Virgil, Wyatt, Morgan, and Warren—were taught at an early age to love the land and above all to respect the law. Wyatt later said that his father had a

> regard for the land [that] was equaled by his respect for the law and his detestation for the lawless elements so prevalent in the West. I heard him say many times that while the law might not be entirely just, it generally expressed the will of the decent folks who were trying to build up the country, and that until someone could offer a

43

A scene from the movie Gunfight at the O.K. Corral, *a Hollywood interpretation of the famous gunfight involving western hero Wyatt Earp.*

better safeguard for a man's rights, enforcement of the law was the duty of every man who asked for its protection in any way.[25]

Nicholas Earp's emphasis on law and order had a strong effect on the Earp boys, and all of them would work as lawmen at some point in their lives.

Bored with life on the family farm, Wyatt Earp left his family in California in the mid-1860s and wandered east in search of adventure. He worked for a time on the railroads and as a scout for wagon trains heading west. Like other young men, Earp learned to be self-reliant while living on the plains of the West. He sharpened his skills as a marksman, earning his living for a time as a buffalo hunter.

First Step to Being a Lawman

Eventually, Earp wandered into Lamar, Missouri, and it was there, in 1870, that Wyatt Earp married his first wife. It was an apparently happy marriage, but it was over almost before it had begun. In 1871, his wife died during a typhoid outbreak.

It was while living in Lamar that Earp took his first steps toward becoming a lawman, running for the office of constable. Earp won the election and might well have remained there but for the death of his wife. The loss of his wife hit Earp hard, and he quit his job and left town.

Earp wandered south into what was at the time Indian Territory (now Oklahoma) and remained for a year. This was a troubled time for Earp, and in his wanderings he got into various sorts of trouble. In 1872, for example, Earp was arrested for horse stealing, but he managed to escape and fled north to Kansas.

Two years after his scrape with the law in Oklahoma, Earp appeared in Wichita, Kansas, where his older brother James owned a saloon and brothel. Soon after his arrival, Wyatt Earp was hired as a deputy marshal. His duties consisted of collecting taxes, a task he found distasteful, and arresting drunken cowboys. Despite being an accomplished marksman, Earp relied on his fists to handle disorderly drunks. He only drew his gun to "pistol-whip" offenders before hauling them off to the town jail. In fact, the only time Earp fired his gun while in Wichita could hardly be described as a gunfight, since he was trying to stop a fleeing horse thief named W. W. Compton. He shot the man in the buttocks.

Wyatt Earp worked as a deputy marshal in the town of Wichita, Kansas, in 1874. This was the beginning of a life in law enforcement.

Earp might have stayed in Wichita had he not gotten into a brawl with a fellow deputy. One night in 1876, Earp was gambling in a saloon and overheard Deputy Marshal William Smith making disparaging remarks about the town marshal, Michael Meager, who was a close friend of Earp's. Earp told Smith to shut up or be ready to fight. Smith, who was drunk, made the mistake of opting to fight, and Earp beat him senseless. Smith filed a complaint against Earp, and the town council removed him from his post. Earp, disgusted at being punished for defending the honor of his employer, left Wichita. He stayed in Kansas, though, and his next stop, Dodge City, would be where he would first make a name for himself.

Earp in Dodge City, Kansas

Dodge City was alternately known as the "Queen of the Cow Towns" and the "Gomorrah of the Plains." Thanks to the cattle business, it was a boomtown where cash was plentiful and where saloons, gambling houses, and brothels flourished, attracting gamblers, prostitutes, gunmen, and thieves of all description. Mayor George M. Hoover had heard of Earp's no-nonsense brand of law enforcement, and soon after Earp arrived in 1876, the mayor made him a deputy marshal, paying him $250 a month plus $2.50 per arrest.

As in Wichita, Earp relied mainly on his fists to keep unruly citizens in line, occasionally pistol-whipping a transgressor into submission. Earp was soon promoted to chief deputy and established what became known as the "Deadline." The Deadline was the railroad track that ran through the middle of Dodge City. Earp prohibited the carrying of any firearms north of those tracks in the "civilized" part of Dodge. Any gunman venturing into this area

Dodge City, of which Earp was the deputy sheriff, was home to a profitable cattle business.

wearing his six-gun was quickly arrested by Earp or one of the other deputies—his younger brother Morgan Earp, William Barclay "Bat" Masterson, or his brother, Jim Masterson.

Earp soon tired of Dodge City, and in the fall of 1876, he turned in his badge. Earp had heard of gold strikes in the Black Hills of South Dakota. With his brother Morgan, Wyatt Earp went north to try his luck prospecting for gold. The venture was short-lived. Wyatt and Morgan Earp returned to Dodge City in May 1877 after the city's new mayor, James H. "Dog" Kelley, wired them and asked them to help control the cowboys who were shooting up the town. Kelley made Wyatt Earp the assistant city marshal.

Soon after pinning the badge on his chest for the second time, Earp was confronted by a group of intoxicated cowboys in front of the Dodge House. They pulled their guns and threatened him, but luckily for Earp, a young dentist and gambler from Georgia who rented out an office on the second floor of the Dodge House leaned out of the window with a shotgun. He aimed it at the cowboys and shouted, "The marshal has his gun put away! Put yours away!"[26] When the cowboys saw the shotgun aimed at them, they holstered their weapons, with the exception of their ringleader. Earp calmly walked up to the man and pulled him down from his horse. Before hauling the troublemaker off to jail, Earp waved up to the young dentist, John Henry "Doc" Holliday. It was the beginning of a lifelong friendship between the two men.

Earp's brand of law enforcement was effective, but eventually it earned him the hatred of both the cowboys and their employers. A $1,000 reward was posted for anyone who killed Wyatt Earp, and it was not long before someone tried to collect it. One night while Earp was standing in front of the Comique Theater in Dodge City, George R. Hoyt emptied his gun at Earp from horseback, missing every time. In response, Earp coolly drew his own gun and fired three times. The first two shots missed, but the third shot struck Hoyt in the forehead and he dropped from his horse. The would-be assassin died a month later.

Earp remained in Dodge City until 1879, when he received a letter from the owners of the Oriental Saloon in Tombstone, Arizona, asking him and his brothers to protect the lavish saloon from the gunmen and thugs employed by rival saloon owners. In exchange, the owners of the Oriental were willing to give Earp a share in the business, worth about $1,000 a month. Tired of the meager pay he received in Dodge City and disgusted by what he saw as the citizens' ingratitude for his efforts on their behalf,

John "Doc" Holliday became a close friend with Wyatt Earp after helping him capture a group of cowboys in the town of Dodge City.

Wyatt agreed to the deal and left for Tombstone with his brother Morgan. The loyal Doc Holliday packed up his guns, cards, and Bowie knife and followed the Earps to Arizona.

Earp in Tombstone, Arizona

Tombstone, Arizona, in the late 1870s was the last of the Wild West towns. Originally established to cater to the miners who were working silver claims nearby, Tombstone quickly attracted the dregs of western society. It was a town in dire need of effective law enforcement. Soon after arriving in Tombstone, Wyatt and Morgan were joined by their brothers Virgil and James, and the brothers wasted no time getting down to business.

Soon after arriving in Tombstone, Wyatt's older brother Virgil became the town's marshal, and Virgil in turn hired Morgan Earp as his deputy. Wyatt went to work as a dealer in the Oriental Saloon, which meant that he could provide security and keep an eye on his share of the business. In addition, Wyatt also worked part-time as a shotgun messenger (the armed guard who rode on stage-coaches) for Wells Fargo and as a deputy U.S. marshal.

As sworn enforcers of the law, the Earps were soon at odds with the Clanton-McLowery gang. The Clanton-McLowery gang was led by Newman H. "Old Man" Clanton and his sons, Ike, Peter, Finn, and Billy. The gang terrorized Tombstone and the surrounding countryside rustling horses and cattle, robbing stagecoaches, and murdering those who opposed them. The gang was aided in its illegal endeavors by a host of gunfighters, including Tom and Frank McLowery, Johnny Ringo, Pony Deal, Pete Spence, Frank Patterson, Billy Claiborne, and Frank Stilwell. Wyatt Earp warned Ike Clanton that the gang's lawlessness would no longer be tolerated in Tombstone.

The Earps began to interfere with the Clantons' rustling activities, which enraged the Clantons and their allies. The gang had been able to operate without fear of arrest by bribing John H. Behan, the sheriff of Cochise County, to look the other way. Aside from being allied with the Clantons, Sheriff Behan had another reason to dislike the Earps. Behan had had a run-in with the Earps' friend Doc Holliday, who spent his days gambling and drinking in the local saloons. The sheriff had accused the dentist of cheating in a game of faro, and Holliday had responded by challenging Behan to a fight. Behan backed down, and Holliday further humiliated the sheriff by taunting him in front of a jeering crowd. From then on, Behan hated both the Earps and Holliday. But the rivalry between Behan and the Earps soon took an even uglier turn.

Battling the Clantons

In March 1881, the Kinnear and Company stagecoach leaving Tombstone was ambushed, and the driver of the stage and a passenger were killed. The stagecoach guard, Bob Paul, managed to outrun the would-be robbers and reach Benson, Arizona. Wyatt Earp, as a deputy U.S. marshal, put together a posse, including Sheriff Behan, to track down the bandits. The posse cornered a small-time thief named Luther King, who confessed that he had taken part in the attempted robbery. King named members of the Clanton gang as participants. While Earp and the posse tried to track the rest of the bandits, Behan returned to Tombstone with the prisoner.

The posse failed to find the other robbers and returned to Tombstone to find that King had escaped. Knowing of Behan's connections to the Clantons, Wyatt Earp accused him of letting King escape. Behan countered by accusing the Earps and Holliday of involvement in the attempted robbery. Holliday laughed off the charge, saying that if he had robbed the stage, he would have shot the horses.

Further evidence of Behan's complicity with the Clantons was to come. In September 1881, the stage bound for Bisbee, Arizona, was robbed of $2,500 in gold. The passengers identified Frank Stilwell, Sheriff Behan's chief deputy, as one of the robbers. Stilwell and another member of the Clanton gang, Pete Spence, were arrested in Bisbee, Arizona, and transferred to Tombstone to stand trial. Predictably, the Clantons—and Ike Clanton in particular—were upset by the arrests.

The feud between the Earps and the Clantons continued. Another member of the Clanton gang, Billy Claiborne, was arrested and charged with murder in Charleston, Arizona, just a few weeks after Stilwell and Spence were arrested. The Clanton-McLowery gang raided the town and freed Claiborne, and Ike Clanton bragged that if the Earps ever jailed one of his men in Tombstone, the same thing would happen there. The citizens of Tombstone realized that the simmering dispute between the Earps and the Clantons would soon boil over into open warfare.

The Coming Fight

Tensions finally came to a head later that autumn. On October 26, 1881, just after midnight, several men, including Ike Clanton and Holliday, gathered in the lunchroom of the Alhambra Saloon for a late-night snack. The intoxicated and armed Holliday confronted Clanton about threats he had made against the Earps, telling him that should they make more threats, they would have him, Doc Holliday, to deal with. Clanton answered with curses, but the confrontation was to get uglier still.

Clanton boasted of his gang's intentions, indicating that he and the rest of the gang were prepared for a fight. As Clanton was speaking, Morgan Earp entered the room. Hearing the remarks, he told Clanton that he was ready for a gunfight on the spot. Clanton spread back the bottom of his jacket to show that he was not armed. Apparently, he was uncertain of Earp's intentions. In a quavering voice he said, "Don't shoot me in the back, will you, Morg?"[27] He then turned and left the lunchroom.

Morgan Earp, Wyatt's brother, was also known for his gunfighting skills and played a large role in the tensions between the Earps and the Clantons, which later resulted in the gunfight at the O.K. Corral.

The Gunfight at the O.K. Corral

At 11:30 A.M. the following day, Wyatt Earp was awakened by Ned Boyle, the bartender at the Oriental Saloon, who had just met Ike Clanton on the street. Clanton had told Boyle, "As soon as those damned Earps make their appearance on the street today, the ball will open."[28] It is unclear at this point whether the Clanton-McLowery gang challenged the Earps to a fight or if the Earps took it upon themselves to arrest the gang, knowing that such a move might provoke a gunfight. In any case, Wyatt, Virgil, and Morgan Earp gathered in front of Hafford's Saloon and began to arm themselves. Carrying a shotgun, Holliday joined the brothers and the four men started down the street in the direction of the O.K. Corral.

Sheriff Behan was getting a shave when he learned about the impending gunfight. He leaped out of the barber's chair and raced to intercept the Earps and Holliday. He told the Earps that he intended to arrest and disarm the Clanton-McLowery gang if they would give him a few minutes alone with them. The Earps ignored Behan and continued walking toward the O.K. Corral. Behan hurried ahead of the Earps and tried instead to persuade the Clanton gang to give up their guns. Ike Clanton insisted he was unarmed, a fact Behan confirmed by feeling around his waist. Tom McLowery opened his vest to show that he was also unarmed. But Billy Clanton and Frank McLowery were armed with revolvers, and a rifle hung in a scabbard on Frank's horse. Behan pleaded with both sides to lay down their weapons, but to no avail.

The two groups stood facing each other in silence. Doc Holliday and Wyatt, Virgil, and Morgan Earp on one side; Frank and Tom McLowery and Billy and Ike Clanton on the other. Frank McLowery and Billy Clanton reached for their guns. The gunfight that ensued lasted less than a minute, and at the end of it, three men, Billy Clanton, Tom McLowery, and Frank McLowery, were dead; three others, Doc Holliday, Virgil Earp, and Morgan Earp, were wounded.

The Aftermath of the Shootout

Although the gunfight at the O.K. Corral was over, the fallout from the shooting was just beginning. Wyatt Earp and Holliday were arrested and charged with murder, while Virgil Earp was discharged from his job as city marshal. After a thirty-day trial, Wyatt Earp and Holliday were found innocent. The judge ruled that the men were acting as "officers charged with the duty of arresting and disarming brave and determined men who were experts in the use of firearms, as quick as thought and as certain as death, and who had previously declared their intentions not to be arrested or disarmed."[29]

The verdict did not end the violence. Two months after the shootout at the O.K. Corral, Virgil Earp was wounded by a blast from a shotgun as he crossed a street in Tombstone. The shot mangled Virgil's left arm, leaving him permanently disabled. The assailant was never caught but was believed to have been an ally of the Clantons. Wyatt was deeply disturbed by the shooting and vowed revenge.

Three months after Virgil was shot, Morgan Earp was shot in the back as he played pool in Hatch's Saloon. Wyatt rushed to his brother's side as Morgan lay dying on the saloon floor. The mortally wounded man tried to be lighthearted about his impending death, saying, "This is the last game of pool I'll ever play."[30]

Morgan died in Wyatt's arms, and Wyatt's resolve to exact vengeance increased. Witnesses told Earp that they had seen four men running from the scene: Pete Spence, Frank Stilwell, Hank Swilling, and Florentino "Indian Charlie" Cruz. All were known Clanton associates.

Three days later, Wyatt Earp and Holliday put the body of Morgan Earp on a westbound train, along with the crippled Virgil Earp, and began the trip to California and the Earps' family home. Wyatt Earp and Holliday, however, got off the train in Tucson, Arizona. There they met up with Wyatt's youngest brother, Warren, and three cohorts: "Texas Jack" Vermillion, "Turkey Creek" Jack Johnson, and Sherman McMasters. Wyatt Earp had received word that Clanton gunmen would attempt to ambush the surviving Earp family members at the Tucson train yards, and he meant to be prepared.

A search of the yards turned up four men, two of whom, Pete Spence and Frank Stilwell, Wyatt Earp shot. Earp and his posse eventually tracked down and killed Florentino "Indian Charlie" Cruz just outside of Tombstone, Arizona. After killing Cruz, both Holliday and Wyatt Earp left Arizona for good.

Wyatt Earp's life after the shootout at the O.K. Corral was uneventful. After leaving Tombstone, Wyatt wandered throughout the West prospecting in the gold camps of Colorado and Idaho. He tried to maintain a low profile, but his notoriety dogged him. Earp was constantly on the lookout for gunmen who wanted to kill him for their own reputations. In an attempt to escape his past, he traveled north to Alaska during the gold rush at the turn of the century and remained there for several years.

Confident that his past was behind him, Earp returned to California in the early part of the twentieth century. Thanks to exaggerated accounts of the shootout at the O.K. Corral, Earp had become a mythic gunfighter, and he found himself not the target of assassins, but of autograph seekers. He pursued several occupations during his later life, including being a consultant on movies about the Wild West, working as a boxing referee in Los Angeles, and raising thoroughbred horses in Del Mar, California. Wyatt Earp eventually became a police officer in Los Angeles, where his reputation as a lawman and a gunfighter meant that he had little trouble enforcing the law: By some accounts, merely identifying himself was enough to cause criminals to surrender, and he never fired his weapon while patrolling Los Angeles. Earp died peacefully in Los Angeles in 1929 at the age of eighty-one.

CHAPTER 5

The Deadliest Gunfighter: John Wesley Hardin

John Wesley Hardin was the most feared gunfighter in the American West. To his admirers, he was the misunderstood victim of oppression. To his detractors, he was nothing more than a cold-blooded killer. Hardin claimed to have killed forty men in stand-up gunfights, and the number may be accurate. Whenever he rode out of town, there was at least one dead man left behind.

John Wesley Hardin was born on May 25, 1853, in Bonham, Texas. His father, James C. Hardin, was a hardworking circuit-riding Methodist preacher. His mother, Elizabeth Dixon Hardin, was described by a family friend as "a cultured woman from an educated and comfortable family"[31] who worked as a schoolteacher. The Hardin name was famous throughout Texas before "Wes" Hardin was born. One of Hardin's forefathers fought at San Jacinto, Texas, in the Texan war for independence. Another had signed the Texas declaration of independence from Mexico. Hardin's grandfather had served in the Congress of the Texas Republic, and Hardin County, Texas, was named after another relative, Judge William B. Hardin. Hardin's father had high hopes for his son and named him after the founder of Methodism, John Wesley. However, neither his religious upbringing nor his illustrious family history had much effect on John Wesley Hardin.

Even as a child, John Wesley Hardin displayed a violent temperament. At about age nine, young Hardin got into a knife fight with an older boy, Charles Sloter. The cause of the fight is uncertain, but what is known is that Hardin attacked the boy with a murderous fury, stabbing him several times before Sloter ran home bleeding from his wounds. Sloter's parents protested to the school board and the sheriff, but Hardin was cleared of any wrongdoing after it was revealed that the Sloter boy was also armed with a knife and had stabbed John Wesley as well.

The Civil War was raging, and Hardin, still only nine, and his cousin Manning Clements ran off to join the Confederate army. They were brought back by Hardin's father, who punished both boys. Hardin later recalled the Civil War years as having a distinct impact on his personality: "The way you bend a tree, that is the way it grows. I grew up a Rebel."[32] Hardin would remain an outlaw for the better part of his life.

By the time Hardin was twelve, he was an accomplished hunter of deer, raccoon, possum, and wildcats. "We all carried guns in those days,"[33] Hardin later remembered. In a frontier world where firearms were accepted as commonplace objects, Hardin still stood apart as being one of the best marksmen in the county.

Hardin's First Gunfights

Hardin's career as a gunfighter began in 1865 when he was visiting an uncle's farm near Moscow, Texas. There, Hardin got into a wrestling match with a former slave named Mage. Mage was older and bigger than Hardin, but Hardin managed to throw him twice. In the second fall, Hardin's ring scratched Mage's face, and the wrestling match deteriorated into a fistfight. Mage was forced to leave by Hardin's relatives. While he was leaving, Mage threatened that "No white boy could draw his blood and live."[34]

John Wesley Hardin's gunfighting life began at the age of twelve when he shot and killed a former slave in Texas.

The next morning, as Hardin was riding home, he encountered Mage on the road. When the ex-slave tried to hit Hardin with a club, Hardin drew his pistol and shot him three times. Hardin rode back to his uncle's plantation and returned with his uncle and several of his relatives. It was obvious Mage was dying from his wounds, and Hardin's uncle sent a nephew to tell Hardin's father about the killing. Hardin's father knew his son was in trouble. Texas at the time was occupied by federal troops. A Southerner, even a boy of twelve, might well be killed by the occupation forces. The elder Hardin sent John Wesley to stay with friends on an isolated ranch until martial law ended and the troops left the state.

From this point, Hardin's life became one incident of bloodshed after another. While hiding out, Hardin heard that a Union patrol was approaching the ranch with the intention of arresting him. He armed himself with a shotgun and a six-gun and waited in ambush. As the soldiers rode past his hiding place, Hardin shot two soldiers with the shotgun and emptied his revolver into the third. Some fellow Texans arrived on the scene and buried the dead Union soldiers while Hardin fled.

Hardin hid among relatives for a few months before reuniting with his father in January 1868 at the Old World School in Pisga, Texas, where Hardin's father was the headmaster. Hardin worked as a substitute teacher for three months, teaching students older than himself the basics of reading, writing, and arithmetic. He proved to be a satisfactory teacher, and the school board offered him a contract for another term, but Hardin turned down the offer.

Instead, Hardin joined his cousins Manning Clements and Tom Dixon in rounding up and selling the wild longhorn cattle that belonged to anyone with the courage to rope them. It was an unrestricted life. The three teenagers spent their days on the plains of central Texas rounding up cattle and they spent their nights in the frontier gambling halls and saloons.

Despite his efforts to abide by the law, Hardin was still a wanted man, and that only led to more trouble. By the fall of 1869, John Wesley Hardin had killed two more Union soldiers who had tried to arrest him. Texas governor Edmund J. Davis publicly vowed to have the young man killed, jailed, or hanged, and he formed the "Texas State Police" in part to help him do just that. Hardin's friends and relatives, however, never failed to warn him when he was in danger of arrest.

John Wesley Hardin was just sixteen but was considered to be the deadliest gunfighter in Texas. He had developed the fastest yet most unusual draw in the West. Instead of drawing from the hip, Hardin had two holsters sewn into his vest so that the butts of his guns pointed inward across his chest. This allowed Hardin to draw and fire his weapons in one sweeping motion. Hardin was not only fast but accurate.

Life on the Run

Hardin's deadly reputation did not prevent other people from taking their chances by challenging him, though. On Christmas Day

1869 Hardin was playing cards in Towash, Texas. In a day-long poker game, Hardin managed to clean out the town tough, Jim Bradley. At one point in the game, Bradley brandished a knife and threatened Hardin: "You win another hand and I cut out your liver, kid."[35] Hardin, who was unarmed, politely excused himself and went to his hotel room, where he strapped on two six-guns.

Hardin returned to the saloon and challenged Bradley to a fight. Bradley strapped on his gun, stepped into the street, cursed Hardin, and fired at him, missing. Hardin's hands flashed across his chest, he drew his guns and fired twice at Bradley. One bullet struck Bradley in the head and the second entered his chest. Bradley died within seconds; Hardin fled the town just ahead of a posse.

The next few months saw Hardin continually on the run, but always deadly. In brief stays in the towns of Horn Hill and Kosse, Texas, a pattern emerged. Hardin would arrive in town, there would be an altercation and an exchange of gunfire, then Hardin would ride out of town with a posse in pursuit.

By late 1870, Texas was getting too hot for Hardin so he decided to go to Louisiana and hide out with relatives there. Before he could get across the state line, however, Hardin was mistaken for another fugitive and arrested in Lake View, Texas. Hardin was quickly identified, and the state police made plans to move him to a stronger jail in Waco, five days away. For $50 and his overcoat, Hardin bought a .45 Colt with four bullets that a fellow prisoner had managed to acquire. Hardin tied the gun under his arm and waited for an opportunity. The opportunity arose on the second day of the trip when he and his guards stopped along the Trinity River to rest for the night. While one of the guards went to a nearby ranch to obtain food for the horses, Hardin shot and killed the other guard and fled on horseback.

Hardin ran to Comanche, Texas, for a brief reunion with his mother and father, who convinced him to go to Mexico. On the road between Belton and Waco, Texas, Hardin was captured by three state policemen. Luck, and the incompetence of his captors, was in Hardin's favor: The officers got drunk that night and passed out. Hardin killed all three as they slept and escaped to the town of Gonzales, Texas.

In Gonzales, Hardin met up with his cousin Manning Clements. The two decided to attend a relative's wedding, and it was there that Hardin met Jane Bowen, the sixteen-year-old daughter of a local rancher. Hardin proposed marriage to the young lady and she accepted on the spot. With at least one aspect of a chaotic life settled, Hardin and his cousin joined a cattle drive to Abilene, Kansas. Hardin promised to return as soon as possible to marry Jane Bowen.

Hardin Goes to Abilene, Kansas

Whatever his skill at handling cows might have been, Hardin's skill with his guns was put to use on the cattle drive. Near the end of the trail, Hardin's boss, a man named William Cohron, was shot and killed by a Mexican vaquero named Juan Bideno. Hardin and two other men, assigned to find the killer, tracked Bideno as he moved south toward Texas.

The three men caught up with Bideno in Bluff City, Kansas, where they found him eating in a small diner. One of Hardin's friends watched the front door and another covered the back door while Hardin walked into the restaurant. Hardin told Bideno to surrender. Bideno smiled and leaned back in his chair so that his holsters were clear. When Bideno attempted to draw his guns, Hardin drew his own weapons and fired twice. Both bullets struck Bideno in the head. Hardin was paid $1,000 for his services, although he later claimed "that at the time I killed him I never expected to receive a cent, and only expected to have my expenses paid."[36]

Once the cattle drive ended in Abilene, Kansas, Hardin joined his fellow cowboys in carousing. Abilene's marshal, "Wild Bill" Hickok, knew of Hardin's reputation, but the two men arranged a truce over drinks. Hardin would be allowed to wear his guns as long as he behaved himself. The truce lasted for several days, and Hardin roamed about the town drinking and gambling but not causing any serious disturbances.

The truce between Hickok and Hardin ended when Hardin shot a man through a wall of the American House Hotel; the man's only offense had been that he was snoring. Hardin looked out the window of the hotel just in time to see Hickok approaching with four other lawmen. Hardin jumped from a window on the second floor of the hotel and hid in a haystack for the rest of the night. Toward dawn he stole a horse and escaped to the cow camps just outside of Abilene and disappeared. Hickok, satisfied that Hardin had left town, decided not to pursue him.

Hardin Returns to Texas

By September 1871, Hardin had returned to Texas. Having heard that two Union soldiers were looking for him, Hardin caught up to the two men in Smiley, Texas, as they were eating cheese and

This illustration from The Life of J.W. Hardin *depicts Hardin's escape from the American House Hotel in Abilene, Kansas, where he killed a man for snoring.*

crackers in a general store. Hardin walked into the store and, reasoning that the troopers would not know what he looked like, engaged them in conversation. The two men confirmed that they were looking for Hardin and that they planned to arrest him. Hardin's response was predictable: "Well, you see him now!"[37]

With that he drew both of his guns and emptied them into the soldiers. He killed one man and forced the other to flee with wounds to his chest and mouth. Hardin fled the town with a fifteen-man posse in pursuit. In the running gunfight that ensued, he managed to kill three more men. The killings in Smiley enraged Governor Davis, who ordered the police to bring Hardin in dead or alive.

An Attempt to Settle Down

After the incident in Smiley, Hardin returned to Gonzales, Texas, to pursue his romance with Jane Bowen. In the winter of 1872, Jane Bowen's father gave his consent for her to marry Hardin, and in March 1872, the couple were wed. Hardin apparently attempted to settle down, and he later insisted that as a married man he tried to avoid strangers who might be seeking to make a reputation for themselves by killing him. A quiet life eluded him, however.

In an attempt to make an honest living, Hardin and his cousin Manning Clements decided to put together a stable of racehorses. In July 1872, the two men rode to Trinity City, Texas, to inspect a mare that was making a reputation at the local racetrack. It was a trip that would have lasting consequences for Hardin. While Hardin and Clements were waiting to meet a relative of theirs in a local saloon and tenpin alley, Hardin got into a bowling game with Phil Sublette, who had a reputation as a gunman. During the game, there was an argument over a wager, and Sublette threatened to kill Hardin. The argument escalated and the events that ensued followed a familiar pattern, but only to a point. Sublette quietly left the saloon and then returned carrying a shotgun.

Someone grabbed Hardin and held him as Sublette fired. The load of buckshot hit Hardin in the stomach. Hardin broke free and, bleeding badly, stumbled toward Sublette. Sublette dropped the shotgun and ran from the saloon. Hardin staggered into the street firing at Sublette as he dodged from house to house. He hit Sublette once in the shoulder before collapsing into the street. The unconscious Hardin was moved to a nearby hotel, where doctors operated on his stomach wound, although they had little hope that he would live. Manning Clements rode off to fetch Hardin's wife.

Hardin did not die, however. A few days after the operation, Clements learned that several state policemen had heard about the shooting and were on their way to arrest Hardin. Despite the protests of the horrified doctors that he would not last an hour, Clements and Jane dressed Hardin, put him on a horse, and rode out of town. The police arrived at the hotel soon after Clements

Manning Clements tried to open a racehorse stable with Hardin during his more peaceful time in Gonzales, Texas.

and Hardin had left and set out in pursuit. In a wild gunfight on the outskirts of town, Hardin managed to kill two of his pursuers, but he received another wound in the thigh. As darkness fell, Hardin and Clements escaped into the hills.

By the following day, Hardin was bleeding profusely from both his wounds. Jane joined the two men in the hills and persuaded Hardin to surrender. Clements then arranged for Hardin's surrender to Cherokee County sheriff Richard Regan, who promised not to turn him over to the state police. A few days later, Hardin, supported by Clements, rode to the rendezvous with Regan. Regan then transported Hardin to the jail at Austin. A jubilant Governor Davis learned of Hardin's capture and predicted that the young gunfighter would soon hang. He then announced plans for the state police to take over the Austin jail. Unwilling to see his cousin hang, Clements bribed Hardin's guards and helped Hardin escape back to Gonzales, Texas. Battered, weakened, and subdued, Hardin promised his wife that he would hang up his guns forever. Again, it was a promise that he would not be able to keep.

The Sutton-Taylor Feud

The vicinity of Gonzales and DeWitt Counties was the scene of a smoldering feud between two families, the Suttons and the Taylors, that had recently erupted into open warfare. The stronger of the two families, the Suttons, had the political blessing of Governor Davis and his state police. The Taylors, on the other hand, were friends of the Clementses and Dixons, who in turn were relatives of John Wesley Hardin, whom they encouraged to join their ranks. Hardin and his wife by this time had two children, both girls, and Jane begged him not to get involved, even though it was difficult for him to stay neutral in such a situation.

Hardin managed to stay clear of the Sutton-Taylor feud, but one day in Cuero, Texas, Hardin was openly challenged by J. W. Morgan, the town's sheriff and a Sutton supporter. Hardin tried to ignore him, but when Morgan tried to take him into custody at gunpoint, Hardin drew his own weapon and killed the sheriff. Hardin rode back to Gonzales, where he discovered that Bill Sutton, the leader of the Sutton faction, had threatened his wife and infant daughters. Enraged, Hardin joined the Taylor family and at a meeting of the clan was chosen as their leader.

The feud continued for almost two years, with many atrocities committed by both sides. Finally, in April 1874, when an innocent bystander, Gabriel "Gabe" Slaughter, was killed in a confrontation between the two families, angry citizens demanded that the new governor, Richard Coke, put an end to the feud. Coke sent the Texas Rangers into DeWitt and Gonzales Counties with orders to quell the fighting. The rangers were given explicit orders to arrest John Wesley Hardin.

Hardin's Last Gunfight

Upon hearing the news, Hardin sent his wife and family to Comanche, Texas, to stay with relatives. Hardin joined his family in Comanche in May 1874. On May 25, 1874, Hardin's twenty-first birthday, Brown County sheriff Charles Webb, who had publicly promised to either arrest Hardin or kill him, rode into Comanche.

Having been tipped off that Webb was coming to town, Hardin was ready for the confrontation. It was race day in Comanche, and large crowds of people were in town to attend the horse races.

The two men first saw each other at the racetrack. Hardin, armed with two six-guns, carefully watched Webb. Manning Clements and the Dixon brothers, all armed, followed Webb through the race-day crowds. The sheriff realized it would be suicide to attempt to arrest or kill Hardin among his friends and family.

Hardin's horses were the best on the track that day, and by the

Richard Coke, Texas governor in 1874, made great efforts to have Hardin arrested after listening to many citizens' complaints about the famous gunfighter.

Hardin's choice of weaponry was the single action army .45 revolver.

afternoon he was $3,000 richer. Accompanied by his brother Joe Hardin, who was a lawyer, and Manning Clements, Hardin went to Joe Wright's saloon to celebrate. Webb followed the three men to the saloon, and Hardin confronted Webb on the wooden sidewalk outside. He spread his coat backward to reveal the jutting gun-butts in his vest holsters and asked if Webb had an arrest warrant. Webb claimed not to know him, and when Hardin introduced himself, Webb told him that he had no warrant. Hardin's reply was direct: "Well, then sir, that settles it. There are no differences between us. Will you join me for a drink and cigar?"[38] Webb agreed, but when Hardin turned his back to enter the saloon, Webb moved to draw his gun. Someone shouted a warning and Hardin spun around, drew his guns, and fired. A single bullet struck Webb in the head.

For a moment there was silence, but then the street erupted with shouts and gunfire. Hardin and Clements managed to fight their way free and rode out of town in a hail of bullets. However, the angry crowd managed to capture Joe Hardin and Hardin's cousins, the Dixon brothers, and they were imprisoned in the Comanche jail. A short time later, a mob of Brown County residents stormed the jail and lynched the three prisoners.

Realizing that he was no longer safe anywhere in Texas, Hardin fled to Florida, then to Alabama, where he became a horse trader, a stockman, and a saloon owner under the name of James W. Swain. Meanwhile, the state of Texas had posted a $4,000 reward for Hardin dead or alive. Dozens of gunfighters, bounty hunters,

Pinkerton (a private detective agency) detectives, and Texas Rangers scoured Texas and the rest of the South for Hardin.

The Texas Rangers finally tracked down the elusive gunfighter and learned that he would be boarding a train in Pensacola, Florida, bound for Alabama. On August 23, 1877, Hardin and an old friend, Jim Mann, boarded a train at the station in Pensacola. They were followed on board by four Texas Rangers disguised as passengers, who took seats behind them. Lieutenant John B. Armstrong of the Texas Rangers boarded next and took a seat across the aisle from Hardin. Before the train began to move, Armstrong stood up, pulled his gun, and pointed it at Hardin's head. When the gunfighter saw the gun, he shouted, "Texas, by God!"[39] and began to reach for his own weapon, but it got tangled in his suspenders. This gave the rangers sitting behind him enough time to disarm and handcuff him. Jim Mann, who was not wanted, jumped from his seat and squeezed off a shot that tore Armstrong's hat from his head. Armstrong fired a shot at Mann that struck him in the chest. The young man did a wild dance in the aisle of the passenger car before diving out a window onto the platform, where he staggered a few steps and died. Hardin was put on a different train, this one bound for Texas. Although Hardin vigorously denied that he was the man the rangers were looking for, he eventually broke down and admitted that he was indeed the infamous gunfighter.

Hardin's Trial, Imprisonment, and Later Life

Hardin went on trial in Gonzales, Texas, for the murder of Deputy Sheriff Charles Webb. Hardin chose to represent himself and amazed everyone in the courtroom with his eloquence. "People will call me a killer, but I swear to you gentlemen that I have shot only in defense of myself. And when Sheriff Webb drew his pistol, I had to draw mine. Anybody else would have done the same thing. Sheriff Webb had shot a lot of men."[40] The jury retired and returned within an hour and a half. Hardin was found guilty of second-degree murder and was sentenced to twenty-five years' hard labor in the Huntsville Prison. John Wesley Hardin was twenty-four years old.

During the first ten years that Hardin was in prison, he attempted to escape many times and led several prison revolts. Eventually, however, Hardin settled down, and he became a model prisoner during his last nine years in prison. He spent his time studying theology and law, filing petitions, motions, and appeals in order to win his freedom. In the process, he earned a law degree.

While Hardin languished in prison, his wife loyally waited for the day he would return. The two were not to be reunited, however. On November 6, 1892, Jane Bowen Hardin died after months of illness. Hardin was stunned by his wife's death and wrote to a friend, "Only Time alone can wash away the tears of [my] grief."[41]

Hardin was pardoned in the spring of 1894 and released into a world that had changed drastically since he was last free. Many of his friends were dead, including his cousin Manning Clements. Hardin's children had grown into adults and were now married with families of their own. Hardin was alone. He was a sick middle-aged man in constant pain from old gunshot wounds and still grieving over the death of the wife who had waited so long for him.

After his release, Hardin established a law office in Gonzales. His business was a modest success, and things seemed to be going his way. In the winter of 1894, Hardin met and courted Callie Lewis, a woman many years his junior. The couple was married, but the relationship lasted for only a month before Lewis returned home to her family. The breakup of his marriage was a shattering blow to Hardin, leaving him deeply embittered and depressed. He began to drink and frequent the gambling halls. He decided it was time to move on.

In early 1895, Hardin moved to El Paso, opened a law office, and, despite his alcoholism, gained a reputation as a good criminal lawyer. In El Paso he met the widow of a rustler named Martin McRose, and he and Mrs. McRose began an intense relationship. One night, Mrs. McRose was arrested for being drunk and disorderly, and Hardin, drunk himself, began to insult the arresting officers, John Selman and John Selman Jr. The elder Selman was not a man to forget an insult, and when he heard that Hardin had been bragging about his intention to settle the score, Selman went looking for Hardin.

The elder Selman found Hardin shaking dice for drinks in the Acme Saloon on the night of August 19, 1895. Selman calmly walked up behind Hardin, drew his gun, aimed, and fired. The bullet took off the back of Hardin's head, but Selman was taking no chances. As Hardin's body lay on the floor, he fired two more shots into the corpse. Selman was arrested and charged with murder but was acquitted on the grounds of self-defense. Hardin's death made headlines all over Texas. The *San Antonio Herald* proclaimed, "Wes Hardin is Killed . . . The Fate of all Bad Killers."[42]

CHAPTER 6

Hollywood's Favorite Bad Man: William H. "Billy the Kid" Bonney

William Bonney has been the subject of countless novels, ballads, and films. Even a play and a ballet were written about his life. Bonney is usually portrayed as either a cowboy Robin Hood or a dim-witted pathological killer. But the portrait that emerges when the records of his life are examined is that of a lonely young man with a misplaced sense of loyalty.

William Bonney was born in New York City on November 23, 1859. Historians disagree about Bonney's real name and parentage. Some argue that Bonney's real name is Henry McCarty and that he was the son of Michael and Catherine (or Kathleen) McCarty. Others argue that he was the son of William and Catherine Bonney (they say that McCarty was Catherine's maiden name) and that William Bonney is his actual birth name. Whatever the case may be, Billy's father died while he was still a small child and his mother moved with him and his younger brother, Joseph, to Indianapolis, Indiana. Mrs. Bonney supported her family by dabbling in real estate, operating a boardinghouse, and doing laundry.

In 1865, Mrs. Bonney met William Antrim, an express company driver, in Indianapolis. Antrim and Mrs. Bonney had a curious romance. Antrim courted his widow sweetheart for more than six years but could not get her to marry him. When Mrs. Bonney decided to move to the rough Kansas frontier town of Wichita, Antrim followed her. In Wichita, Mrs. Bonney continued to deal in real estate and to take in laundry.

In the late spring of 1871, Mrs. Bonney abruptly stopped dealing in real estate and sold all of her property. A physician had told her that she had tuberculosis and urged her to move to a drier climate. Mrs. Bonney, with her two children and Antrim in tow, moved to Silver City, New Mexico, where she opened a boardinghouse. In

1873, Mrs. Bonney finally agreed to marry William Antrim, and the couple was married on March 1 in the First Presbyterian Church in Santa Fe, New Mexico. A little over a year later, however, Catherine Bonney Antrim was dead.

Watching his mother die greatly affected William Bonney. At age thirteen, he refused to attend school and began to spend his time gambling. William Antrim tried to discipline Bonney, but the boy became more uncontrollable by the day. Antrim eventually allowed Bonney to go to work for the Star Hotel in Silver City. Bonney worked there for a year waiting tables and doing kitchen chores. He adopted the owner, Mrs. Truesdell, as a surrogate mother, and she warned him that his association with Silver City toughs would only lead to trouble. Many years later, when Mrs. Truesdell was asked about William Bonney, she remembered him as a polite and well-mannered boy who worked hard and never stole anything.

William Bonney (Billy the Kid) began a life of gambling at the young age of thirteen.

Bonney's First Brushes with the Law

Mrs. Truesdell's prediction came true in September 1875. William Bonney was arrested as the result of a practical joke. He and an older boy, known only as "Sombrero Jack," stole some clothes from a Chinese laundry. Bonney was placed in jail to await punishment, but he escaped by climbing up the chimney. Bonney went to the home of Mrs. Truesdell and told her what had happened. Truesdell took pity on the boy, fed him, gave him some money, and put him on the stagecoach to Globe, Arizona. She never saw him again.

What Bonney did or where he went over the next two years remains a mystery, but Bonney turned up in Grant City, Arizona, in 1877. There, Bonney managed to get a job with the U.S. Army as a civilian teamster and quickly became known around town as "the Kid." It was at this time that Bonney's life changed radically, and not for the better, when he killed his first man in Grant City. The victim was a blacksmith named E. P. Cahill, also known as

"Windy," who was fond of bullying Bonney. An eyewitness to the event described what followed:

> One day he [Cahill] threw the youth [Bonney] to the floor. Pinned his arms down with his knees and started slapping his face. "You are hurting me. Let me up!" cried the Kid. "I want to hurt you. That's why I got you down," was the reply. People in the saloon watched the two on the floor. Billy's right arm was free from the elbow down. He started working his hand around and finally managed to grasp his .45. Suddenly silence reigned in the room. The blacksmith evidently felt the gun in his side for he straightened sharply. There was a deafening roar. Windy slumped to one side and the Kid squirmed free and ran to the door and vaulted into the saddle of John Murphy's racing pony and left for Fort Grant.[43]

Wanted for the murder of Cahill, Bonney drifted through the cow and mining camps of Arizona and New Mexico gambling, drinking, and working at odd jobs. He eventually found his way into Lincoln County, New Mexico, where the legendary aspects of the life of "Billy the Kid" began.

Lincoln County, New Mexico

The populace of Lincoln County at this time was divided between two competing factions. On one side was L. G. Murphy and Company, commonly called "the Company," and on the other was the group known as the Tunstall-McSween faction. The Company had been founded by Major Lawrence G. Murphy and Lieutenant Colonel Emil Fritz. The two men quickly established a monopoly in Lincoln County selling ranching supplies, dry goods, and cattle. In an attempt to drive smaller ranchers from its lands, the Company began to charge the ranchers high prices for goods and high interest on any credit transactions.

The Company's activities were protected by the Santa Fe Ring, a group of corrupt politicians who controlled prosecuting attorneys, judges, sheriffs, and deputies throughout the New Mexico Territory. The day-to-day running of the Company was left to Jimmy Dolan, an Irish immigrant who had become indispensable to Murphy for his skill with account keeping, and Jimmy Riley, another Irish immigrant who had bought his way into the Company with an investment of $6,000. Dolan and Riley employed a gang of gunfighters to intimidate the small ranchers and to protect the Company's vast land and cattle holdings.

The other faction was headed by John Tunstall, an Englishman who had established a cattle ranch at the headwaters of the Rio Feliz, and Alexander McSween, an idealistic lawyer who attempted to combat the Company in court and advised Tunstall on legal matters. Tunstall, who had a reputation for honesty, established a store in Lincoln and began to sell goods to the ranchers at lower prices than the Company did. This caused many small ranchers to transfer their accounts to his store. The competition put the Company in financial difficulty and soured relations between the two factions. Caught between the two factions were the small ranchers, who had been organized into a loose confederation by one rancher, Dick Brewer.

It was into this charged environment that William Bonney wandered when he arrived in Lincoln County during the fall of 1877. He first went to work for the Company as a cowboy, but after an argument with his foreman, he packed his gear and left. Some weeks later, Bonney rode onto the Coe ranch in the beautiful valley of the Rio Ruidoso and found work as a ranch hand. It was at the Coe ranch that Bonney met Dick Brewer. Brewer described to Bonney how he and his fellow ranchers were being victimized by the Company and how the Tunstall-McSween faction was attempting to set things right. Brewer revealed the confrontations between the ranchers and the Company's gunmen and predicted that the tensions would soon become open warfare.

Dick Brewer introduced William Bonney to John Tunstall, who immediately hired Bonney to work on his ranch. Years later, Frank Coe recalled that meeting: "Tunstall saw the boy was quick to learn and not afraid of anything. . . . He made Billy [Bonney] a present of a good horse, saddle and a new gun. . . . My, but the boy was proud . . . said it was the first time in his life he had ever had anything given to him."[44] In the same way that Bonney had adopted Mrs. Truesdell as a surrogate mother, he adopted the cultured Englishman with his strange accent and extensive library as a surrogate father.

One day when Bonney was helping Frank Coe on the ranch, Coe witnessed a demonstration of Bonney's skill with a sixshooter. Bonney pointed to a row of birds sitting on a branch, and as Frank Coe remembered, he never saw Bonney draw, but he did see the birds tumble off their perch. Coe also remembered Bonney as lighthearted, recalling that he was "always joking and full of tricks."[45] But Bonney had another side, and he could be moody, withdrawn, and thoughtful at times.

As tensions between the Company and the Tunstall-McSween faction grew, Bonney's friends on the Tunstall and Coe ranches noticed a tense alertness about him. He still laughed and delighted in flirting with the local girls, but Bonney's blue eyes would suddenly become cold and hostile when strangers approached the Tunstall spread or when he escorted Tunstall on the long ride into Lincoln. It would not be long before events would change Bonney's life forever.

The Beginning of the Lincoln County War

The ill feelings between the Company and the Tunstall-McSween faction gradually escalated with a series of legal maneuvers. When the Company obtained a court order for the seizure of Tunstall's livestock, the Lincoln County sheriff sent a hastily assembled group of deputized gunfighters to execute the order. When the "deputies" arrived at the Tunstall ranch, they discovered that Bonney and the ranch hands had barricaded themselves inside and were ready to shoot it out with the deputies. The deputies left but promised to return.

The next day, Tunstall, having decided that he would turn the cattle and the horses over to the deputies and seek justice in the courts, returned to the ranch from Lincoln and ordered Bonney and the others to leave. Bonney urged Tunstall to defend his ranch and property, but Tunstall refused. The following day, Tunstall and his ranch hands, Bonney, Fred Waite, Dick Brewer, Bob Widenmann, and John Middleton, headed to Lincoln with nine horses that were the personal property of the ranch hands and not included in the court order.

Shortly after Tunstall and the cowboys left, a group of deputies led by Jimmy Dolan arrived at the ranch. Tunstall's cook, Godfrey "George" Gauss, told the men that his boss and the ranch hands had left for Lincoln, taking nine horses with them. Dolan selected a dozen riders, placed them under the leadership of a man named Billy Morton, and ordered them to retrieve the horses. It was almost dark when Morton's posse caught up to Tunstall and his cowboys. Here is what happened in Bonney's own words:

> When we had traveled about thirty miles . . . and just upon reaching the brow of a hill we saw a large party coming toward us from the rear at full speed. Middleton and I rode forward to warn the balance of the party. We had barely reached Brewer and Widenmann who were some 200 or 300 yards to the left of the trail when the attacking party cleared the brow of the hill and began firing at us. With

Widenmann and Brewer I rode over the hill toward another hill which was covered with large rocks and trees so we could defend ourselves and make a stand. But the attacking party, undoubtedly seeing Tunstall, left off pursuing us to turn back to the canon [canyon] in which the trail was. Shortly afterwards we heard two separate and distinct shots. The remark was made by Middleton that they, the attacking party, must have killed Tunstall. . . . Neither I or any member of the party fired either rifle or pistol.[46]

After Morton and the deputies rode off, Bonney ordered Brewer, Middleton, Widenmann, and Waite to ride to Lincoln to inform McSween about Tunstall's death while he rode to the Coe ranch to find someone to retrieve Tunstall's body. When Bonney arrived at the Coe ranch later that night, he told Frank Coe of Tunstall's death. Coe listened as Bonney explained the events of that afternoon. After he had finished his story, Bonney swore that he would kill every man who had any connection with Tunstall's death. The Lincoln County War was on.

The Lincoln County War

Over the next six months, Bonney and a group of men—known as the Regulators—roamed Lincoln County engaging in numerous skirmishes with Company gunfighters. Although both groups had been deputized and were supposed to be enforcing the law, they were little more than vigilantes. The Lincoln County War resulted in at least a dozen deaths, many under suspicious circumstances.

For example, at the beginning of the war, Bonney killed the two men, Billy Morton and Frank Baker, whom he held responsible for Tunstall's murder. About a month later, Bonney and a group of Regulators slipped into Lincoln and ambushed Sheriff Brady and two of his deputies as they walked down the street. The Regulators managed to kill the sheriff and one of his deputies but were forced to flee when the third deputy summoned help.

Perhaps the most sensational moment of the war was what came to be known as the "Battle of Lincoln." The Regulators, led by Bonney, and a contingent of Mexican vaqueros barricaded themselves in the McSween house and another building nearby with the intention of protecting McSween and his family from the Company's gunmen. The Mexican vaqueros took over the nearby Montano building to protect the Regulators in the McSween house from a rear attack. The Company responded by surrounding both buildings with gunmen, supported by thirty U.S. cavalry troopers, a cannon, and a Gatling

Bonney and his friends, known as the Regulators, played a major role in the Lincoln County War as Bonney sought revenge for the death of John Tunstall.

gun. The siege lasted eight days and left several Regulators wounded and one Company gunman dead. On the night of the eighth day, Company gunmen managed to set fire to the McSween house. Bonney, McSween, and the Regulators fled through the back door and were met by gunfire. In the brief fight in the darkness, McSween was killed. With both Tunstall and McSween dead, the Lincoln County War was officially over, but Bonney was not done fighting. Moreover, the violence was far from ended.

The Aftermath of the Lincoln County War

Bonney and a ragtag band of men, mostly veterans of the Lincoln County War, began to steal livestock from ranchers in the area. The band worked out of Fort Sumner, New Mexico, where Bonney had many friends who would feed and shelter them. One of the friends who fed and sheltered Bonney and his band during this time was Pat Garrett, a Fort Sumner bartender and cowboy who had befriended Bonney. The two men spent many nights together drinking and attending local dances.

In November 1878, based on an investigation he had conducted, the territorial governor, Lew Wallace, proclaimed a general amnesty for crimes committed during the Lincoln County War; however, the amnesty did not apply to anyone currently under indictment. This meant that Bonney was still a fugitive because he was under indictment for the murder of Sheriff Brady.

Over the next year and a half, Bonney dealt with the aftermath of his involvement in the Lincoln County War. A temporary truce between Bonney and the Company's men ended only in more violence and the death of another ally of McSween and Tunstall. The territorial governor once lured Bonney into a situation where he could be captured, but he managed to escape before he could be put on trial.

The Manhunt for Bonney

During the summer of 1879, Bonney and his friends made their headquarters in Beaver Smith's Saloon in Fort Sumner, New Mexico. They drifted through the country along the Pecos River working on ranches, gambling, drinking, and racing horses. For the most part, Bonney and his riders avoided trouble, but wherever Bonney went, violence soon followed.

In January 1880, Bonney claimed his next kill, Joe Grant, a young tough who had sworn to kill him. In a confrontation in a saloon, Bonney tried to cajole Grant out of a fight, but the drunken gunslinger drew his gun and fired at Bonney. Grant's shot missed, but Bonney's did not.

By April 1880, Bonney had been joined by new companions who were drawn to him by his reputation or because they were also on the run. Joining Bonney and his friend Tom O'Folliard were "Doc" Scurlock, Dave Rudabaugh, Billy Wilson, Tom Pickett, and Charlie Bowdre. The men remained in the Fort Sumner area for the rest of the year, pursuing women, gambling, and drinking. During the summer of 1880, Bonney's old friend Pat Garrett was appointed deputy sheriff of Lincoln County and deputy U.S. marshal. Despite the urging of his superiors, Garrett delayed going after Bonney.

The Company's gunmen used a Gatling gun when they surrounded Bonney and the Regulators during the Lincoln County War.

Finally, during the winter of 1880, Garrett, spurred on by superiors who threatened to fire him and backed by a posse of gunfighters, began to move against Bonney. Garrett and his men tracked Bonney and his companions through the bitterest winter in the history of the New Mexico Territory. The two groups of gunfighters accidentally ran into each other in Fort Sumner, New

Mexico, on December 19, 1880, when Bonney led his men into town for supplies. The two groups exchanged gunfire and Garrett killed O'Folliard but Bonney and the rest of the gang fled.

The next day, Garrett and his men tracked Bonney through newly fallen snow to an abandoned stone house near Fort Sumner. Garrett's men surrounded the house and waited for someone to come out. Charlie Bowdre was the unlucky one to emerge first and he was shot on sight. Bowdre managed to stagger back into the house before he died. To prevent Bonney's escape, Garrett's men killed one horse and set two others free. Rudabaugh, Wilson, Pickett, and Scurlock convinced Bonney that the only option was to surrender. Reluctantly, Bonney agreed, and the men surrendered to Garrett, who took them to Santa Fe and imprisoned them.

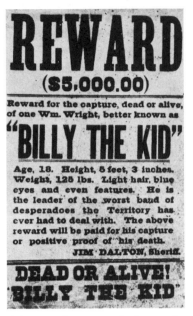

A wanted poster declares the handsome reward of $5,000 for the capture of Billy the Kid.

On Trial for His Life

Bonney's trial in April 1881 took one day. He was found guilty of murdering Sheriff Brady. There was little sympathy for the young outlaw, and the presiding judge sentenced Bonney to hang.

As Garrett began to assemble the materials necessary for the execution, Bonney was returned to his cell to await the fateful day. Bonney was watched over by two guards, Robert Ollinger and J. W. Bell. Ollinger, who had been a Company gunfighter during the Lincoln County War, kept prodding Bonney with his shotgun and taunting him, saying, "I can save you from the hangman, Kid. Just make a run for it. . . . I'd love to put a load of buckshot in your back . . . give it to you the way you gave it to Sheriff Brady."[47] Bonney said nothing and bided his time waiting for the right moment.

One Last Escape

On April 18, 1881, Bonney, in handcuffs and leg irons, asked Bell to help him to the latrine. As Bell was helping him down the stairs to the outhouse in back of the jail, Bonney knocked Bell down and hopped into the gun room, which was next to the stairs. Bonney snatched up a pistol, and Bell pleaded with him to put it down. Bonney, unmoved by the pleas, killed the deputy.

Whether he felt the need to prevent pursuit or just wanted revenge is unclear, but he then retrieved Ollinger's shotgun and waited for Ollinger to come out of the saloon across the street. When Ollinger, drawn by the gunfire at the jail, emerged from the saloon, Bonney greeted him in a friendly voice and then fired both barrels into the lawman, killing him. Bonney then broke the shotgun and threw the pieces at the dead body, saying, "Take it, damn you! You won't follow me any more with that gun."[48] Bonney laughed and danced on the balcony of the jail, then went back inside and armed himself. He forced the jail's janitor to break off his handcuffs and leg irons with a pickax. He then took a horse from the corral behind the jail and escaped.

Bonney's Death

William Bonney fled back to Fort Sumner, New Mexico. Although friends urged him to go south into Mexico while he still had the chance, Bonney ignored their pleas and stayed on in Fort Sumner. Garrett, hearing that Bonney was still in the Fort Sumner area, went there in search of Bonney.

On the night of July 13, 1881, Garrett visited Pete Maxwell, a local businessman, to ask if he had seen Bonney. While Garrett went inside to speak with Maxwell, who was in bed, his companion, John Poe, remained outside on the porch. Soon after Garrett entered the home, the shadowy figure of William Bonney approached the house. Bonney spied Poe and immediately drew his gun and pointed it at him, asking in Spanish, "Quien es? [Who is it?]"[49] He continued to ask the same question over and over as he backed toward the door and entered the darkened house. Apparently unaware that Garrett was also in the house, Bonney asked Maxwell who was outside. Garrett, recognizing Bonney's voice, drew his revolver and fired twice, killing Bonney.

William H. Bonney, alias Billy the Kid, was placed in a cheap pine box and buried in the old military cemetery of Fort Sumner next to his friends Tom O'Folliard and Charles Bowdre. The graves are marked by a simple headstone with the inscription "Pals."

CHAPTER 7

The Last Gunfighter: Tom Horn

Although some gunfighters fought in defense of others, most did so only for personal gain. Tom Horn's name is unfamiliar today, but in his own time he was known as a fearless, some said mad, killer. His execution in 1903 marked the end of the age of the gunfighter and a change in public opinion about the violence and lawlessness of the American West. Until that time it had been acceptable for a man to resort to his gun to defend his property or the property of others. Horn's death heralded the coming of the idea that justice should be meted out by the authorities rather than by professional gunfighters.

Information about Horn's childhood is scanty, but it is known that he was born on November 21, 1860, in Memphis, Missouri. His mother "was a powerful woman . . . a good old fashioned Campbellite [a Christian religious sect],"[50] and his father was a prosperous farmer and a strict disciplinarian. Horn's early life was shaped by his mother's religious fervor and his father's iron-fisted sense of discipline, which dictated that he punish his son severely for the slightest infraction. As a teenager, Horn began to drift away from his parents' beliefs and began to get into more trouble at home. He liked the outdoors and became an expert hunter. He hated school and was often truant, which earned him the anger of his father. One day when Horn was fourteen years old, his father gave him such a severe whipping for truancy that he left home. Horn headed west and never returned.

Horn made his way to Arizona, working on the railroads, driving wagons for a freight company, and eventually driving stagecoaches. Once in Arizona, Horn worked as a cowboy on various ranches, spending time with Mexican vaqueros. While Horn was working as a night herder on a ranch near Camp Verde, Arizona, he became friends with the Apache who lived in the area. By the time he left a year later, Horn was fluent in both Apache and Spanish.

Horn's Career as a Scout

Tom Horn's ability to speak Apache led him to a job as an interpreter on the San Carlos Apache Reservation.

It was Horn's ability to speak Apache that led to his next job. Horn met Al Sieber, a famous Indian scout, in 1876, and Sieber hired him to work as an interpreter on the San Carlos Apache Reservation. The job did not last long, however. When it was discovered that civilian employees of the government were siphoning off funds meant for the Native Americans, all civilians were banned from the reservations. Horn, along with Sieber, lost his job.

Horn, Sieber, and another man, Ed Scheflin, drifted to Tombstone, Arizona. While Sieber worked a mining claim the men had staked out, Horn worked as a hunter, supplying the mining camps with venison for the sum of $2.80 a deer. Before long, however, in October 1876, Sieber and Horn were called to Fort Whipple to join the Sixth Cavalry as scouts. An Apache war chief, Geronimo, had left the reservation, and it was the army's job to bring him back. For the next few months, Sieber and Horn worked with the cavalry, but when the federal funds for civilian scouts ran out in the spring of 1877, Sieber and Horn were laid off.

Three years later, in May 1880, the Chiricahua Apache, led by Geronimo and Chief Nana, again broke out of the reservation. They killed an Indian agent and his Native policeman and cut down the telegraph poles that served as the only means of communication between the reservation and the outside world. Horn, who was working a mine near the reservation, rode thirty-two miles to Fort Thomas to warn the army. During the ensuing conflict, Horn again served as a scout for the cavalry. Eventually, the army was able to gain the upper hand, and Geronimo and his braves agreed to return to the reservation.

For the next five years, Horn continued to work as a scout and an interpreter for the army, eventually rising to the rank of head scout. His fluency in Apache and ability to negotiate with the Native Americans proved invaluable to his government employers.

Then in the summer of 1885, after a tiswin (corn beer) binge, Geronimo led a large number of warriors out of the reservation and into Mexico. General George Cook, the Sixth Cavalry's commander, ordered Captain Emmett Crawford to track down the wily war chief. Horn, as head scout, accompanied the expedition across the border to seek out the runaway band and return them to the reservation.

In January 1886 on the Aros River in Mexico, Horn and his scouts found Geronimo's camp. While the troopers were engaging the Apache, both groups were attacked by Mexican irregulars, and in the fighting, Captain Crawford was killed. Horn convinced the Apache to join him in a temporary alliance, and together the troopers and the Apache drove off the Mexican force. After the battle, a group of Apaches surrendered to Horn and were escorted across the border into the United States. Geronimo, however, remained free.

Horn pursued the Apaches, led by Geronimo, into Mexico.

In April 1886, General Nelson A. Miles replaced General Cook. Miles, confident that his troopers could track the Apache without the help of civilian scouts, dismissed all the scouts, including Horn and Sieber. The dismissals proved shortsighted and costly. The Apache, under Geronimo's leadership, raided with impunity, killing ranchers and Mexicans, kidnapping children, butchering cattle, and stealing horses across southern Arizona. Without the help of the scouts, Miles's troopers failed time and again to catch the elusive Apache.

Miles eventually realized that he needed experienced scouts and asked Sieber and Horn to return. Sieber, by now crippled with rheumatism, refused. But Horn agreed, leaving the mine he was working near Tombstone, Arizona, and returning to the army. This time Miles's men, guided by Horn, kept up a relentless pace chasing the Apache into the mountains. At last Geronimo asked for a meeting with his opponents. The accounts of Geronimo's final surrender vary. Miles insisted that Geronimo surrendered on his own initiative; Horn claimed that it was he who persuaded Geronimo and Chief Nana to surrender.

Horn's Career with the Pinkerton Detective Agency

With the Apache war over, Horn left the army and returned yet again to mining. A peaceful career as a miner was not in his future, however. In 1890, drawn by the pay and the excitement of hunting men, Horn joined the Pinkerton Detective Agency tracking down bank and train robbers. His guns and marksmanship proved a lethal combination as he pursued his quarry throughout Colorado and Wyoming. During his time as a Pinkerton detective, he reportedly killed seven men. Ironically, Horn's most memorable feat as a Pinkerton detective ended not in a killing but with the peaceful capture of the train robber "Peg Leg" Watson.

Watson had been preying on trains in Colorado and southern Wyoming, robbing the passengers and looting the mail cars. After trailing Watson for several weeks, Horn located him in a mountain cabin near Hole-in-the-Wall, Wyoming. Horn yelled to Watson that he was coming for him, and Watson stepped out of the cabin with a six-gun in each hand. Watson watched, open-mouthed, as the six foot, seven inch Horn walked across an open field, his Winchester rifle at his side. Watson never fired a shot, and Horn took him to jail without a struggle. Horn's bravery in facing an armed train robber was heralded across the West, and he became an instant celebrity. But the publicity did not suit Horn, and he quit the Pinkerton Agency in 1893, saying simply, "I haven't the stomach for it anymore."[51]

Horn the Man Hunter

Horn did have the stomach, however, to go to work as a hired gun for the Wyoming Cattle Growers' Association (WCGA). The WCGA was at war with the homesteaders who were flooding Wyoming and setting up farms and ranches on land that the WCGA perceived as its own, even though it was open range. Although there is no indication that Horn participated in the one-sided battle known as the Johnson County War, he did help assemble the mercenary army that attacked and slaughtered homesteaders in the bloody conflict.

Working for the cattlemen suited Horn, and in 1894, he went to work for the Swan Land and Cattle Company as a stock detective. Horn's duties included tracking down and killing rustlers and harassing homesteaders who were settling on and fencing what had been open range. At this time, the term *rustler* was loosely defined. A rustler could be a cattle or horse thief as well as a homesteader who was occupying land that the cattle barons considered their own.

Horn demanded, and received, $600 for each "rustler" he killed, and he proved to be a methodical and ruthless hunter. Horn's lethal procedure became routine. He would spend several days tracking a man, learning his habits, and observing him making camp each night. Finally, Horn would lay a careful ambush and kill his target using a high-powered rifle. Horn was no longer the Indian scout or Pinkerton detective who faced his adversaries in a fair fight. He killed from hiding and killed often. More than a dozen rustlers were found shot to death on the open range. As a sort of "calling card," Horn left his victims lying with a large rock under their heads.

Horn's killing of William Lewis was typical. Lewis was suspected by his neighbors of stealing cattle. Arrested and indicted on rustling charges, Lewis managed to delay his trial on legal technicalities; when his case did finally make it to court, the jury acquitted him on all charges. On July 31, 1895, shortly after Lewis was found innocent, he was loading a skinned calf into a wagon when three .44-caliber slugs tore through him. He was found the next day with a rock under his head. The killing bore all the earmarks of Horn's work, but Horn was never charged with the crime.

Horn Returns to Wyoming

After a brief stint in the army during the Spanish-American War, Horn was back in Wyoming by 1900 and working again as a stock detective. One of the first people he was paid to kill was a rustler named Matt Rash. Horn tracked Rash to his cabin near Cold Springs Mountain in Routt County, Colorado. On July 8,

1900, posing as a prospector named James Hicks, Horn approached the cabin and the unsuspecting Rash invited him to join him for dinner. Following the meal, Horn excused himself, went outside, and hid behind a tree. When Rash stepped outside, Horn pumped three bullets into him, then mounted his horse and rode over one hundred miles to Denver to set up an alibi. Rash lived long enough to write the name of his killer with his own blood, but because he wrote that the assailant was named Hicks, Horn was not immediately identified as the killer.

Horn's next victim was Isom Dart, a cowboy who was suspected of being Rash's partner in rustling. Dart emerged from his Routt County hideout on the morning of October 3, 1900, to inspect his stolen cattle. As he approached the cattle pens, Horn, hidden behind a rock, fired two shots from a .30-.30 rifle, piercing Dart's head. A coroner later said that he found the spot where Horn had fired from and had paced off the distance to Dart's body: It was 196 paces (approximately 163 yards), an incredible feat of marksmanship considering the quality of weapons at the time.

The cattle barons were satisfied with Horn's efforts. Cattle rustling was under control, and the homesteaders were intimidated, leaving the barons' herds free to wander the open range without interference. That winter Horn hung up his rifle and waited for spring—and the opportunities that the new year would bring.

However, the world was rapidly changing around Tom Horn and the Wyoming cattle barons. In 1890, the federal government had declared the frontier "closed," which meant that there was no more land available to homesteaders. The Wild West existed only in isolated pockets of Arizona, New Mexico, Wyoming, Montana, Idaho, and Alaska. The telephone had replaced the telegraph as a means of communication, and millions of people were leaving the countryside for the employment opportunities of the rapidly industrializing cities. Power no longer came from wealth earned from livestock or agriculture but was instead based on money invested in large corporations. The Native American population had been decimated and forced onto reservations; the buffalo were almost extinct; railroads crisscrossed the plains, tying the East and West Coasts together; and the law of the gun was quickly becoming a thing of the past since improved law enforcement made it unnecessary for men to defend their property by themselves.

The Murder of Willie Nickell

America had become a different place, but Horn attempted to earn his living in his accustomed way. On the morning of July 18,

1901, Horn was laying in wait for Kels P. Nickell, a small rancher who had been marked for death by the cattle barons because he had introduced sheep onto the open range. Horn had seen Nickell only once, from a distance, so he did not know that the figure who emerged from the ranch house wearing Kels Nickell's hat and coat was actually Nickell's fourteen-year-old son, Willie.

Willie Nickell was hitching horses to the wagon as he was preparing to leave to spend the night with his father watching over their sheep. When he got down from the wagon to open the gate that led out of the ranch yard, Horn fired a shot that knocked the boy off his feet. Nickell stood up and attempted to climb back into the wagon, but a second shot from Horn struck him in the head, killing him. Mrs. Nickell did not hear the shots, and Willie's body was not discovered until the next day, when it was found by his two younger brothers. Footprints showed that the killer had left his hiding spot, examined the body, and then ridden away.

Willie Nickell's death outraged the small ranchers and farmers in Wyoming, and they demanded that the murderer be brought to justice. The state of Wyoming offered a $500 reward for information leading to the arrest of the killer. Although this killing was immediately attributed to Horn, he denied the charge, claiming that he had been on a train between Laramie and Cheyenne, Wyoming, on the day of the killing. Sensing that Wyoming was becoming too hot for him, Horn traveled to Denver to wait for the storm to blow over.

The uproar over Willie Nickell's killing eventually subsided, but Joe LeFors, the U.S. marshal in Cheyenne, continued to investigate the boy's murder and Horn's possible involvement. Horn was warned that LeFors was asking questions about him, but he ignored the warning and refused to leave town, continuing to make nightly tours of Denver's saloons.

While Horn was carousing in Denver, LeFors visited Laramie, Wyoming, to check on Horn's alibi. In Laramie, LeFors learned that, on the day of the murder, Horn had arrived in town not by train as he had claimed but on a horse that had obviously been ridden hard. Furthermore, LeFors learned that Horn had left a blood-stained sweater at a cobbler's shop. Satisfied that he had identified Willie Nickell's killer, the marshal decided to set a trap for Horn.

LeFors rode to Denver and, posing as the friend of a Montana rancher who was in need of Horn's "services," he got Horn drunk in a small saloon. Between drinks and chews of tobacco, Horn bragged about one of his exploits in which he claimed to have been paid "twenty-one hundred dollars for killing three men and shooting five times at another." His next boast proved to be his undoing. He calmly described in detail how he had killed the Nickell's boy at three hundred yards. He then described the killing as "the dirtiest trick I have ever done."[52] Behind a nearby door in the saloon, LeFors's deputies listened to the conversation and a court stenographer wrote down everything Horn said. After Horn left, LeFors swore out a warrant and Horn was arrested. He was then transported back to Cheyenne, Wyoming, to stand trial.

Horn's Trial and Execution

Horn's trial in the fall of 1902 was one of the most sensational of its time. Although Horn was being tried for murder, it was also clear that an underlying issue was the fight between wealthy cattle barons and the small homesteaders and ranchers. As one historian has said, "It was the old century colliding with the new."[53] The cattle barons provided Horn with the best defense money could buy, and people from all over the country flooded into the small, dusty Cheyenne courtroom for a glimpse of the famous bounty hunter.

Testifying during the trial, LeFors detailed how he had gone about collecting evidence against Horn and how he had set a trap for him. Horn denied that he killed the Nickell's boy and insisted that LeFors had doctored the evidence so that he could collect the reward offered by the state of Wyoming. On the morning of October 23, 1902, the jury returned a verdict of guilty. Horn was sentenced to hang. He was returned to his cell while his appeals worked their way through the courts. The question of Horn's guilt was replaced by a new question. People wondered if Horn, in order to save his own life, would betray the cattle baron who had paid him to kill Nickell.

While Horn waited for his date with the executioner, a plot to blow up the jail was uncovered in December when five sticks of dynamite were found in the snow by a wall outside the jail. Rumors circulated through the Cheyenne saloons that other gunmen were plotting a raid to free Horn, but the stories had no basis in fact and the winter and spring passed without incident.

Then in August 1903, Horn and Jim McCloud, who was awaiting trial for robbery, made a desperate escape attempt. McCloud feigned being ill, and when a deputy entered the cell that McCloud shared with Horn, the two men pounced on the deputy and tied him up. The two men then forced the deputy to tell them where the keys to the jail and the gun room were. The deputy explained that the keys were locked in a safe and that he would have to be untied to open it. McCloud and Horn fell for the trick and untied the deputy, who opened the safe. But instead of producing the keys, the deputy retrieved a gun stored there and shot McCloud, slightly wounding him. The two men overpowered the deputy and took the gun away from him, but the gunfire had already attracted the attention of the townspeople and other deputies. McCloud grabbed a shotgun, fled to the corral of the jail, secured a horse, and rode west out of town. Horn, armed with the deputy's pistol, fled through the front door of the jail and was spotted by O. M. Eldrich, who operated a business across the street. Arming

Tom Horn and his trial remain a memorable part of American history.

himself, Eldrich gave chase and fired at Horn several times, one of his bullets grazing Horn's neck. Eldrich was just about to shoot Horn again when the fugitive surrendered.

Horn was returned to his cell, but the city was tense. Rumors of a planned jailbreak persisted, and it was said that a gang of Horn's cowboy friends was gathering outside Cheyenne and preparing to storm the jail. In anticipation of a jailbreak, residents carried shotguns and six-shooters. Kels Nickell, the father of Willie Nickell, paced up and down in front of the jail with a shotgun, telling anyone who would listen, "Let Horn make another break for it and I'll blow his head off . . . he's going to hang if I have to stay here for the rest of my life."[54] Wyoming's governor, Fenimore Chatterton, finally called out the state militia to patrol the town. As Horn's execution neared, armed soldiers and Gatling guns guarded the entrance to the jail, and dozens of armed deputies were stationed in the windows of the courthouse.

By November 1903, thousands of people had arrived in Cheyenne hoping to witness the execution of the West's last gunfighter. The sheriff warned the public to stay away from the site of the execution and instituted security measures to limit the number of witnesses and spectators. With all of his appeals denied, Horn was marched to the scaffold on the morning of November 20, 1903. Despite speculation to the contrary, he spurned requests that he become an informer and name the cattle barons who had paid him to commit murder.

As the rope was placed around his neck, Horn was asked if he had any last words. Horn looked at the gathered crowd, gazed at his sweetheart, Glendolene Kimmel, then turned back to the executioner and said, "Hurry it up. I got nothing more to say."[55] The trapdoor was opened and Horn's neck was broken by the sudden fall. After Horn was declared legally dead, his body was cut down, placed in a coffin, and taken to Boulder, Colorado, for burial.

Horn's execution marks the end of the age of the gunfighter and the end of the public's tolerance for wanton violence in the West. Professional gunfighters, men who killed for money, honor, and reputation, were no longer tolerated. The West, like the rest of the country, was quickly becoming a place where people saw no need for the "law of the gun" when justice could be administered by the courts and professional law enforcement officers. Horn, a leftover from the Old West, had no place in the new West of the twentieth century. Glendolene Kimmel, the schoolteacher who loved Horn, summed up his life when she wrote, "Riding hard, drinking hard, fighting hard—so passed his days, until he was crushed between the grindstones of two civilizations."[56]

NOTES

Chapter 1: America's Westward Expansion

1. Quoted in Richard Maxwell Brown, "Violence," in Clyde A. Milner, Carol O'Connor, and Martha Sandweiss, eds., *The Oxford History of the American West.* New York: Oxford University Press, 1994, p. 395.

2. Quoted in Brown, "Violence," p. 395.

3. Quoted in James D. Horan, *The Gunfighters: The Authentic Wild West.* New York: Crown, 1976, p. 156.

4. Quoted in Joseph G. Rosa, *Age of the Gunfighter: Men and Weapons on the Frontier 1840–1900.* Norman: Oklahoma University Press, 1993, p. 20.

5. Quoted in Rosa, *Age of the Gunfighter,* p. 20.

6. Quoted in Rosa, *Age of the Gunfighter,* p. 107.

7. Quoted in Rosa, *Age of the Gunfighter,* p. 106.

Chapter 2: The Prince of the Pistoleers: James Butler "Wild Bill" Hickok

8. Quoted in Horan, *The Gunfighters,* pp. 87.

9. Quoted in Horan, *The Gunfighters,* p. 96.

10. Quoted in Horan, *The Gunfighters,* pp. 102–103.

11. Quoted in Horan, *The Gunfighters,* p. 103.

12. Quoted in Horan, *The Gunfighters,* p. 103.

13. Quoted in Rosa, *Age of the Gunfighter,* p. 110.

14. Quoted in Geoffrey C. Ward, *The West: An Illustrated History.* Boston: Little, Brown, 1996, p. 279.

15. Quoted in Rosa, *Age of the Gunfighter,* p. 176.

16. Quoted in Rosa, *Age of the Gunfighter,* p. 202.

Chapter 3: The Gunfighter's Gunfighter: Ben Thompson

17. Quoted in Horan, *The Gunfighters,* p. 123.

18. Quoted in Horan, *The Gunfighters,* p. 135.

19. Quoted in Horan, *The Gunfighters,* p. 138.

20. Quoted in Horan, *The Gunfighters,* p. 142.

21. Quoted in Horan, *The Gunfighters,* p. 142.

22. Quoted in Horan, *The Gunfighters*, p. 148.

23. Quoted in Horan, *The Gunfighters*, p. 148.

24. Quoted in Horan, *The Gunfighters*, p. 151.

Chapter 4: Hollywood's Favorite Lawman: Wyatt Berry Stapp Earp

25. Quoted in Jay Robert Nash, *Encyclopedia of Western Lawmen and Outlaws*. New York: Da Capo Press, 1994, p. 110.

26. Quoted in Nash, *Encyclopedia of Western Lawmen and Outlaws*, p. 113.

27. Quoted in Nash, *Encyclopedia of Western Lawmen and Outlaws*, p. 118.

28. Quoted in Paul Trachtman, *The Old West: The Gunfighters*. Alexandria, VA: Time-Life Books, 1974, p. 25.

29. Quoted in Trachtman, *The Old West*, p. 33.

30. Quoted in Trachtman, *The Old West*, p. 34.

Chapter 5: The Deadliest Gunfighter: John Wesley Hardin

31. Quoted in Horan, *The Gunfighters*, p. 155.

32. Quoted in Horan, *The Gunfighters*, p. 156.

33. Quoted in Horan, *The Gunfighters*, p. 155.

34. Quoted in Trachtman, *The Old West*, p. 175.

35. Quoted in Nash, *Encyclopedia of Western Lawmen and Outlaws*, p. 144.

36. Quoted in Horan, *The Gunfighters*, p. 165.

37. Quoted in Nash, *Encyclopedia of Western Lawmen and Outlaws*, p. 145.

38. Quoted in Nash, *Encyclopedia of Western Lawmen and Outlaws*, p. 147.

39. Quoted in Nash, *Encyclopedia of Western Lawmen and Outlaws*, p. 148.

40. Quoted in Nash, *Encyclopedia of Western Lawmen and Outlaws*, p. 148.

41. Quoted in Horan, *The Gunfighters*, p. 182.

42. Quoted in Horan, *The Gunfighters*, p. 185.

Chapter 6: Hollywood's Favorite Bad Man: William H. "Billy the Kid" Bonney

43. Quoted in Horan, *The Gunfighters*, pp. 16–17.

44. Quoted in Horan, *The Gunfighters*, p. 19.

45. Quoted in Horan, *The Gunfighters*, p. 21.

46. Quoted in Horan, *The Gunfighters*, p. 29.

47. Quoted in Nash, *Encyclopedia of Western Lawmen and Outlaws*, p. 44.

48. Quoted in Trachtman, *The Old West*, p. 190.

49. Quoted in Horan, *The Gunfighters*, p. 77.

Chapter 7: The Last Gunfighter: Tom Horn

50. Quoted in Horan, *The Gunfighters*, p. 222.

51. Quoted in Nash, *Encyclopedia of Western Lawmen and Outlaws*, p. 166.

52. Quoted in Horan, *The Gunfighters*, p. 242.

53. Horan, *The Gunfighters*, p. 242.

54. Quoted in Horan, *The Gunfighters*, p. 247.

55. Quoted in Nash, *Encyclopedia of Western Lawmen and Outlaws*, p. 167.

56. Quoted in Horan, *The Gunfighters*, p. 240.

FOR FURTHER READING

Frank Bergon and Zeese Papanikolas, eds., *Looking Far West: The Search for the American West in History, Myth, and Literature*. New York: New American Library, 1978. This 476-page book contains a variety of essays about the American West. It covers topics such as Native American culture, European colonization, the decimation of the Native population, America's westward expansion, mountain men, gunslingers, cowboys, and the role of women on the frontier. This book contains some pictures and is recommended for readers of all ages.

Royal B. Hassrick, *Cowboys and Indians: An Illustrated History*. New York: Promontory Press, 1976. This well-illustrated book covers a wide range of topics dealing with the West, including gunfighters and outlaws. It contains information on such famous figures as Billy the Kid, Belle Starr, and Wild Bill Hickok as well as information on lesser characters like Judge Roy Bean, Charles Goodnight, and Oliver Loving.

Robin May and Joseph G. Rosa, *Gun Law: A Study of Violence in the Wild West*. Chicago: Contemporary Books, 1977. A well-written and researched book, it examines the origins and tradition of violence in the American West. It covers topics such as feuds, outlaws, lawmen, the role of saloons and gambling in fueling violence, and how the violence is portrayed in popular films. An interesting book with many pictures, it is recommended for all readers.

Kent Ladd Streckmesser, *The Western Hero in History and Legend*. Norman: Oklahoma University Press, 1965. This is an interesting book that studies the four hero traditions in American western history: the mountain man (Kit Carson), the outlaw (Billy the Kid), the gunfighter (Wild Bill Hickok), and the soldier (George Armstrong Custer). For each of the categories, a brief biography of a historical figure is given, along with two opposing viewpoints on the person's importance to history and his contribution to the western myth. Recommended for the serious researcher.

———, *Western Outlaws: The "Good Badman" in Fact, Film, and Folklore*. Claremont, CA: Regina Books, 1983. Although the book gives biographical information about outlaws, it is a study of the impact that western outlaws have had on American culture. It contains interesting ideas, a few pictures, and is meant for the serious student of western history.

Brad Williams, *Legendary Outlaws of the West*. New York: David McKay, 1976. This is a nicely written book intended for a young adult audience. It contains black-and-white pictures as well as information on such desperadoes as Joaquin Murieta, Black Bart, Thomas E. Ketchum, and Tom Bell. The biography of each of the outlaws is given in a semifictional narrative.

Works Consulted

James D. Horan, *The Gunfighters: The Authentic Wild West*. New York: Crown, 1976. This is an excellent and reliable source of information on the West's most notorious gunmen. The majority of information is drawn from eyewitness accounts, government records, affidavits, and other legal documents as well as accounts by the gunfighters themselves. The book covers Billy the Kid, Wild Bill Hickok, Ben Thompson, John Wesley Hardin, Tom Horn, Kid Curry, and Harry Tracy.

Clyde A. Milner, Carol O'Connor, and Martha Sandweiss, eds., *The Oxford History of the American West*. New York: Oxford University Press, 1994. This college textbook contains a variety of essays written by the editors and others. It contains many pictures and current information and ideas on the American West. Although the language in places is difficult, it is a must for the serious researcher.

Gary B. Nash and Julie Roy Jeffrey, *The American People: Creating a Nation and a Society*. New York: HarperCollins, 1996. This is a basic college textbook that covers the course of American history. It is easy to read, informative, and contains many pictures. Any person doing research on aspects of American history should consult this book for dates and facts.

Jay Robert Nash, *Encyclopedia of Western Lawmen and Outlaws*. New York: Da Capo Press, 1994. This is a comprehensive reference book covering the full range of western outlaws and lawmen (as well as other characters). It is nicely written and contains biographical information on various historical figures from the Old West. In places, legends are portrayed as facts, but overall, the book is well documented and researched. This book is recommended for anyone with an interest in the American West.

Richard Patterson, *Historical Atlas of the Old West*. Boulder, CO: Johnson Books, 1985. Although this book does not contain much biographical information on gunfighters, it does provide interesting information on specific historical sites throughout the western United States. It contains many pictures and maps and is recommended for readers of all ages.

Harold Rabinowitz, *Black Hats and White Hats: Heroes and Villains of the West*. New York: Friedman/Fairfax, 1996. This book is lavishly illustrated with photographs, paintings, and sketches. It examines the lives of more than forty individuals from different segments of frontier society, including outlaws, lawmen, soldiers, Native Americans, and women. It is easy to read and entertaining.

Joseph G. Rosa, *The Gunfighter: Man or Myth?* Norman: Oklahoma University Press, 1969. This book examines the role that the gunfighters played in the taming of the Wild West and the impact that gunfighters have had on western culture. It contains few pictures and is geared toward serious researchers and students. It is well written but should only be attempted by readers with an advanced vocabulary.

————, *The West of Wild Bill Hickok*. Norman: Oklahoma University Press, 1982. This is a scholarly and in-depth examination of the life of Wild Bill Hickok. It contains many pictures of Hickok throughout his life as well as information on his family, friends, enemies, firearms, and the places he visited. It is highly recommended for anyone with an interest in Hickok, although it can be difficult to read in places.

————, *Age of the Gunfighter: Men and Weapons on the Frontier 1840–1900*. Norman: Oklahoma University Press, 1993. This book contains many photographs, paintings, and sketches. Many of the photographs are of firearms from the Old West. The book is filled with information about many of the West's most notorious gunfighters, as well as information on the firearms of the time. Highly entertaining and factual, this book is recommended for all readers, especially those with an interest in firearms.

————, *Wild Bill Hickok: The Man and His Myth*. Lawrence: Kansas University Press, 1996. This seems to be an update of Rosa's earlier biography of Hickok. Although this book contains fewer pictures than the previous biography, it contains more factual information and examines how Hickok became a larger-than-life figure during the late 1800s and early 1900s. It attempts to separate fact from fiction when it comes to Hickok's real-life exploits. Recommended for the serious Hickok scholar.

Paul Trachtman, *The Old West: The Gunfighters*. Alexandria, VA: Time-Life Books, 1974. This book provides biographical information on the West's most famous (and infamous) gunfighters. It contains many pictures, and the information is accurate and well documented. The author does a good job of putting the role of the gunfighter into historical perspective. The book is easy to read and is recommended for all ages.

Geoffrey C. Ward, *The West: An Illustrated History*. Boston: Little, Brown, 1996. This book is the companion piece to Ken Burns's documentary on the American West. It is well researched and contains a variety of information about different aspects of western history. The book covers such topics as the Native Americans and their role in American history, the Mormons and their trek west, miners, loggers, the expansion of the railroads, and the buffalo hunters. Although the book contains little information on gunfighters, it is highly recommended for the serious scholar or the casual reader. It also contains many previously unpublished photographs.

Picture Credits

Cover photos: center: Photofest; clockwise from top right: The Kansas State Historical Society; Archive Photos; Western History Collections, University of Oklahoma; Western History Collections, University of Oklahoma

Archive Photos, 16, 36, 45, 50, 61, 72

Art Resource, 27

Corbis / Bettmann, 73

The Kansas State Historical Society, 14, 20, 24, 29, 33, 38, 39, 46, 48, 60

Library of Congress, 15

North Wind Picture Archives, 12, 22, 71, 77

Photofest, 9, 44, 66

Texas State Library & Archives Commission, 58

Western History Collections, University of Oklahoma Libraries, 54, 62, 76, 83

About the Author

Thomas Thrasher teaches English at California State University, Long Beach, and Rio Hondo College in Whittier. He lives in Long Beach with his cat Jinx and surfs whenever he gets the chance.